★ ★ ★
TORONTO
Blue Jays

JAMES R. ROTHAUS

CREATIVE EDUCATION

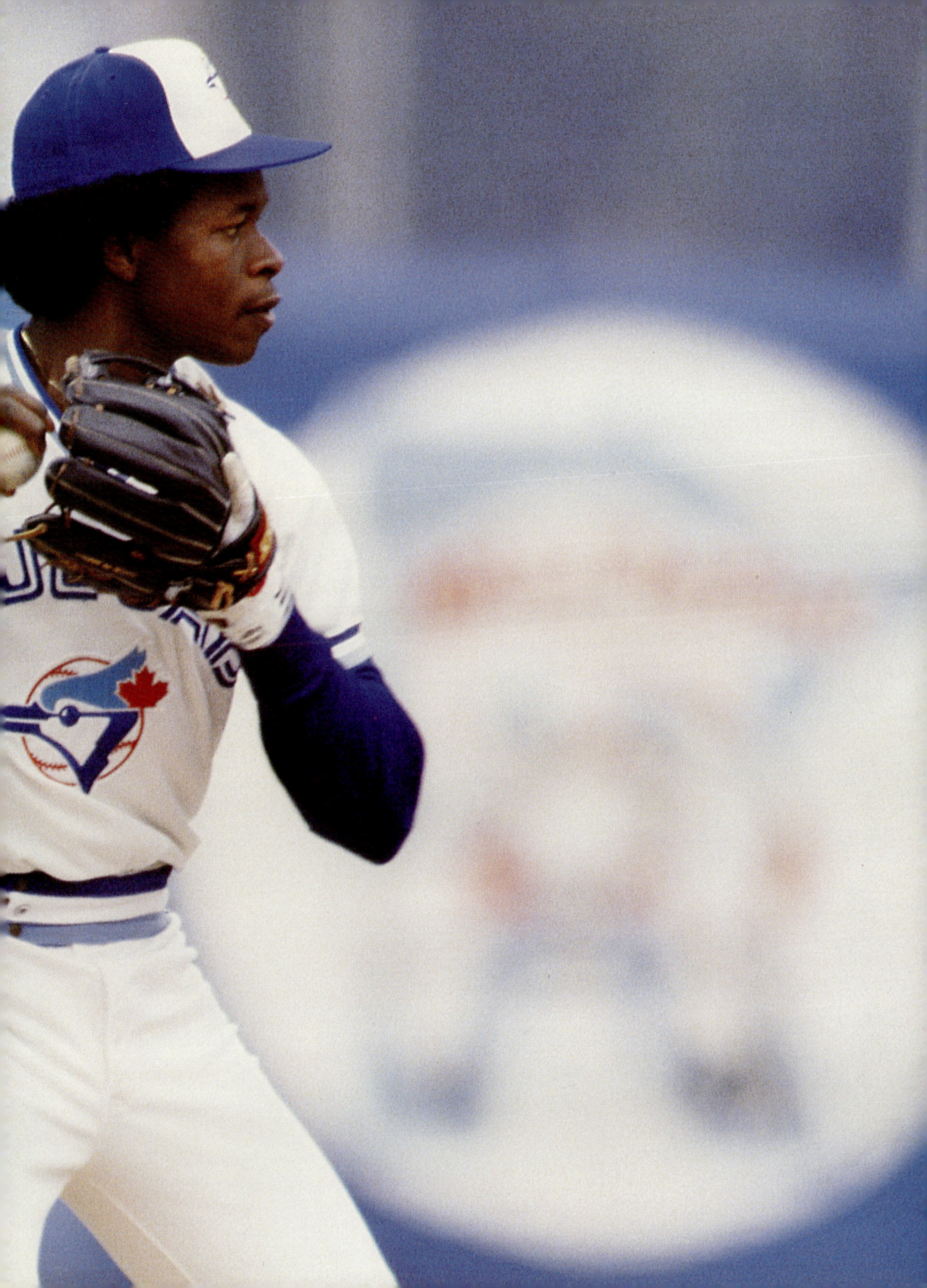

Library of Congress Cataloging-in-Publication Data

Rothaus, James.
  Toronto Blue Jays / James R. Rothaus.
    p. cm.
  ISBN 0-88682-153-3

    1. Toronto Blue Jays (Baseball team)   I. Title.
GV875.T67R68   1987
796.357'64'09713—dc19

★ ★ ★
CONTENTS

The Blue Jays Are Hatched	8
Bavasi Sets The Tone	11
The First Toronto Roster Takes Shape	13
Second-Year Squabbles	19
The Turnaround Begins With Bobby Mattick (1980)	23
Bobby Cox Begins His Magic Act (1982)	30
Toronto Power Surge Jolts A.L. East!	33
Jays Glimpse Championship On Horizon	36
Champs At Last	39
So Much Talent!	41

COVER PHOTO
George Bell has good reason to smile as he watches one of his 31 homers sail away in 1986.

PHOTO SPREAD (PAGE 2/3)
Tony Fernandez sets up to cut down the runner in '86.

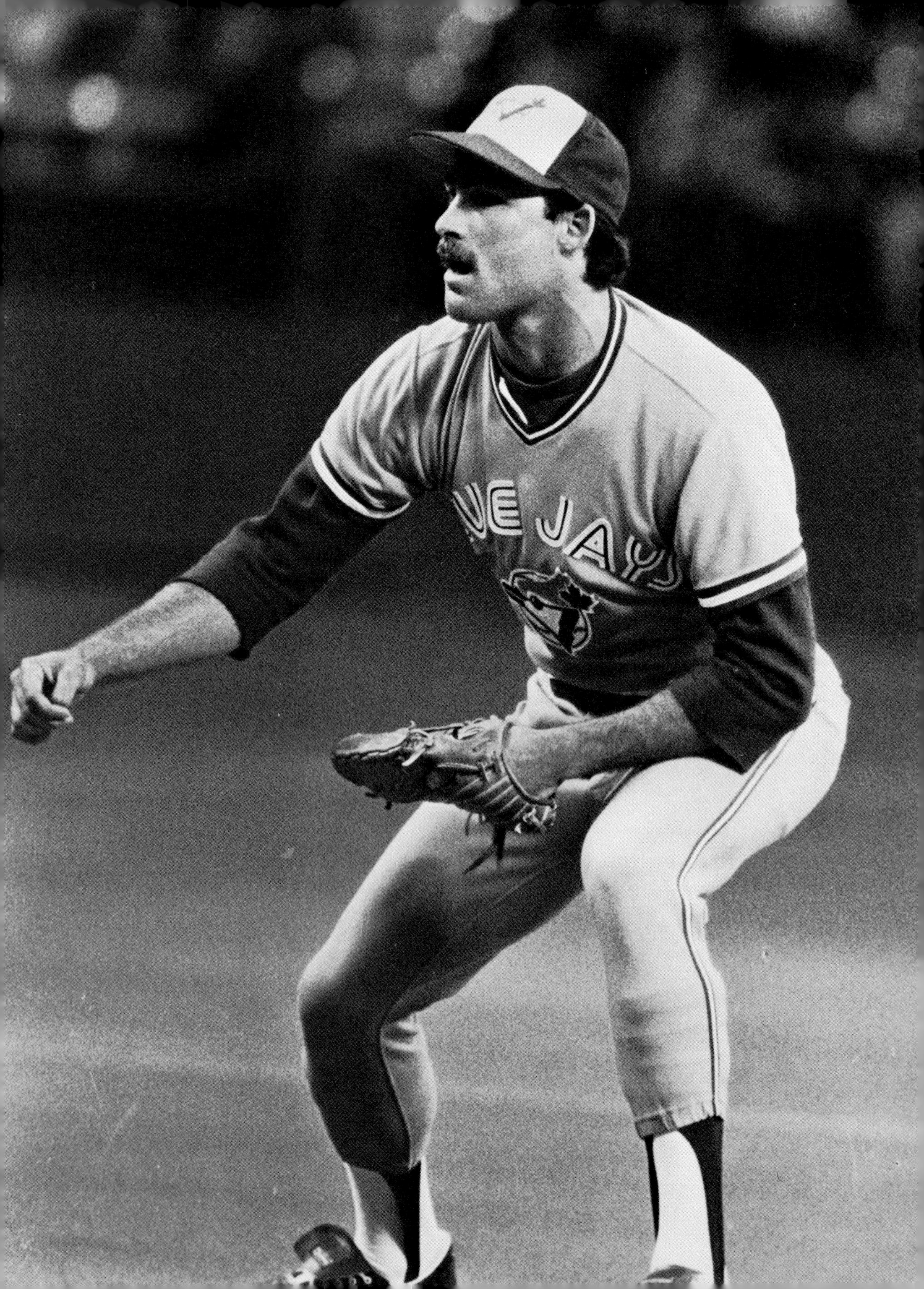
UE JAYS

Centuries ago, travel was long and hard in the untamed land the settlers called America. Even by water, down the St. Lawrence River and across the five Great Lakes, a pioneer's journey to the fertile Midwest could take weeks or months longer than planned.

Those delays were more than inconvenient — they could be deadly. The longer the trips, the greater the chance for illness, injury or some other disaster. The settlers looked for every possible shortcut.

In the early 1700's, the French discovered that the Iroquois Indians used such a shortcut. It was a 75-mile portage, or overland route, northward that saved hundreds of miles in the journey from the first lake, Ontario, to the third, Huron.

Soon, travelers by the thousands used the portage. The French set up a mission, a fur-trading post and a fort at the beginning of the path. A settlement grew at this important site. It was named Toronto, from the Indian word for "meeting place."

In early 1976, Toronto once again became the "meeting place," when a dedicated group of Canadian businessmen gathered to discuss the purchase of a major league baseball club for their great city. Toronto already boasted an exciting professional hockey club — the Maple Leafs — and a pro football club called the Argonauts. But the Toronto sports fans yearned for baseball, too.

Already, a Canadian rivalry was taking shape. In 1969, the Montreal Expos had become the first Canadian major league team. Montreal is the only Canadian city larger than Toronto. When Montreal got its baseball team, the people of Toronto felt a little twinge of jealousy. They set out to get their own ball club. It would not be an easy task.

**March 26, 1976
The American League approves a new expansion club for Toronto. Imperial Trust, Ltd. and Labatt's Breweries pony up most of the $7-million franchise fee.**

**PHOTO
Looking in. Dave Stieb checks his pitch in a 5-0 win over the Mariners. (1980)**

7

Oct. 26, 1976 Toronto G.M. Peter Bavasi arranges the purchase of catcher Phil Roof's contract from the White Sox, officially making Roof the first Blue Jay.

PHOTO Moseby gets a welcome. After a booming homer against Milwaukee, Lloyd Moseby is congratulated by manager Bob Mattick. (1981)

The Blue Jays Are Hatched

In early 1976, investors in Toronto came to an agreement with Horace Stoneham, owner of the N.L.'s San Francisco Giants. The investors would pay $13.25 million to Stoneham and move the Giants to Toronto.

While baseball fans in Toronto celebrated, however, San Francisco was putting up a fight. San Francisco mayor George Moscone got a court order against the sale. Then baseball's commissioner, Bowie Kuhn, got into the act. He put a hold on franchise moves.

The Toronto investors were trying to figure out what to do. Stoneham decided for them. He sidestepped the problems by selling the Giants to other San Francisco investors.

That left Toronto empty-handed, but good news was just ahead.

On March 26, 1976, the American League voted to expand its ranks by two teams, one in Seattle, Washington, and one in Toronto.

Three Canadian companies got together to pay Toronto's $7-million franchise fee. Wealthy financier R. Howard Webster and his company, Imperial Trust, Ltd., bought 45 percent. Labbatt's Breweries also bought 45 percent. The Canadian Imperial Bank of Commerce chipped in the final 10 percent.

The egg had hatched. The Blue Jays were born. A few ruffled feathers had to be put into place, however, before the young Jays would be ready to take their first flight in public. That job fell to the club's first General Manager—Peter Bavasi.

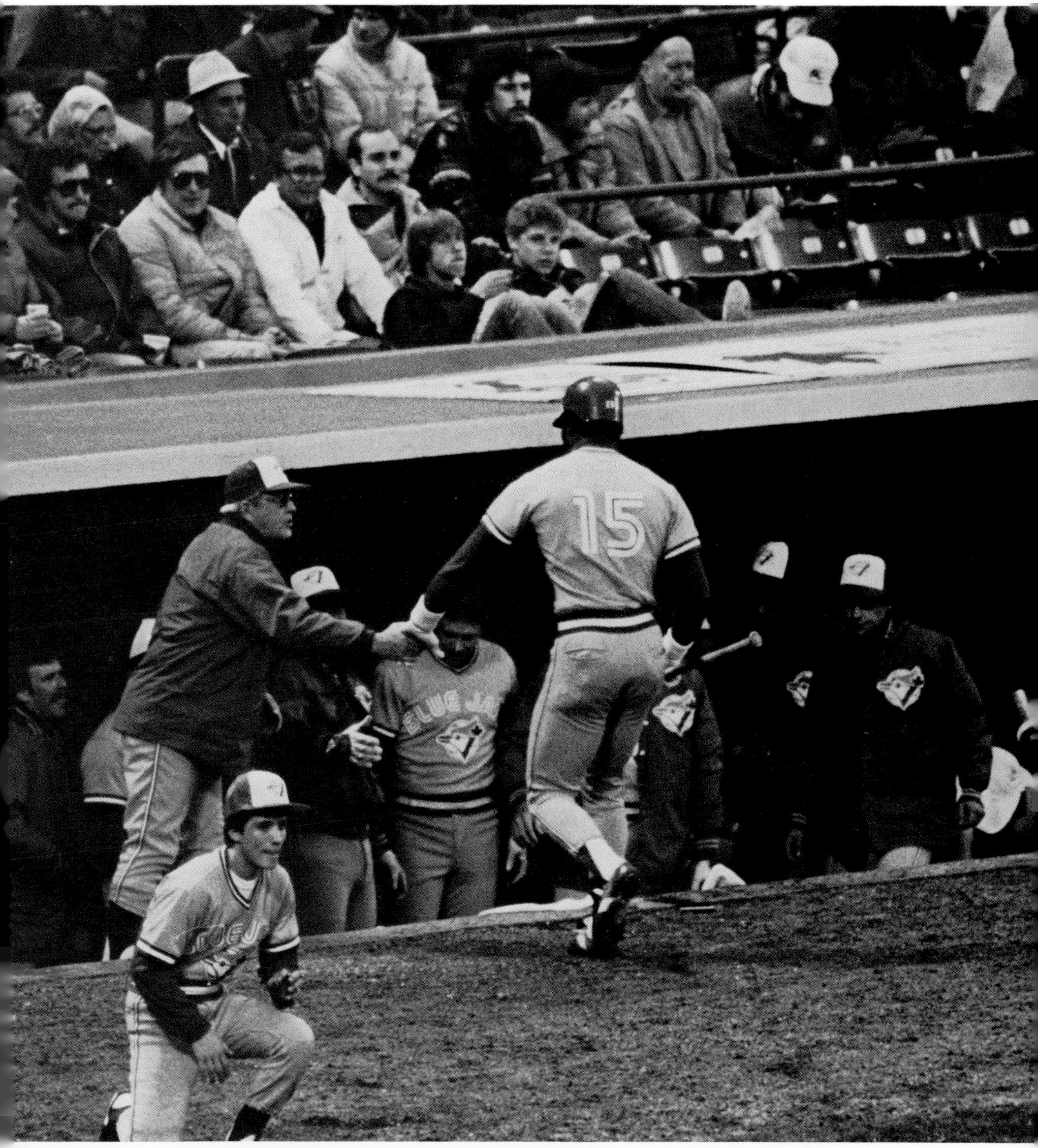
15
BLUE JA

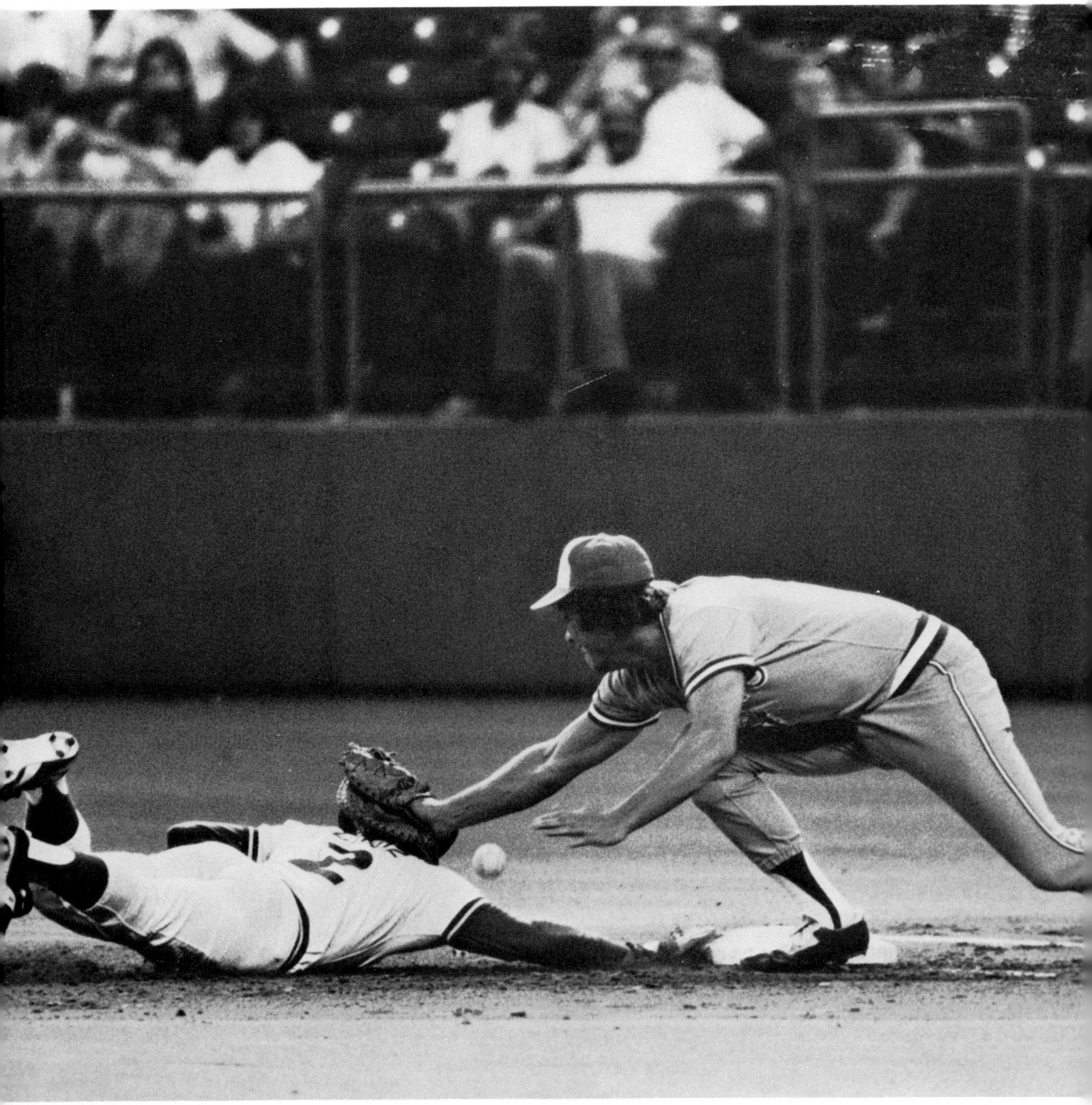

Bavasi Sets The Tone

Peter Bavasi wasn't new to baseball. His father, Buzzie Bavasi, had already left his mark in the front offices of many clubs, including the Brooklyn and Los Angeles Dodgers, the San Diego Padres and the California Angels.

Young Peter Bavasi grew up around baseball. Even as a kid he showed signs of his future career. Most of his friends would watch the ball players and dream about being pros someday. But Peter was fascinated by the concessions — the hot dog stands, the pennant sales, the popcorn vendors. Peter grew up dreaming of running his own supermarket.

As he moved from club to club with his father, Peter learned the business end of baseball from the ground up. He sold tickets. He painted bleachers. He did all the things behind the scenes that help keep a club running smoothly.

Finally, at age 34, he was named Executive Vice President and General Manager of the Blue Jays.

It was Bavasi who set the tone for the early Blue Jays. He worked 18 hours a day to make the team the best it could be. Still, he knew he couldn't push his club too far, too fast.

"You realize the importance of patience when you handle a team like ours," he once said. "If you draft young, as we did, you have to bite the bullet. You don't make wholesale changes. If you do, you wind up mixing and matching — and eventually rebuilding."

Though Bavasi didn't expect the young Jays to win the American League pennant in their first few years, he did have other expectations.

April 7, 1977
Doug Ault hits two homers to spark the Blue Jays to a 9-5 victory over the White Sox in the opening day game of the very first season in Exhibition Stadium.

PHOTO
Toronto's Doug Ault puts a tag on Seattle's Julio Cruz. The ball squirted free. (1978)

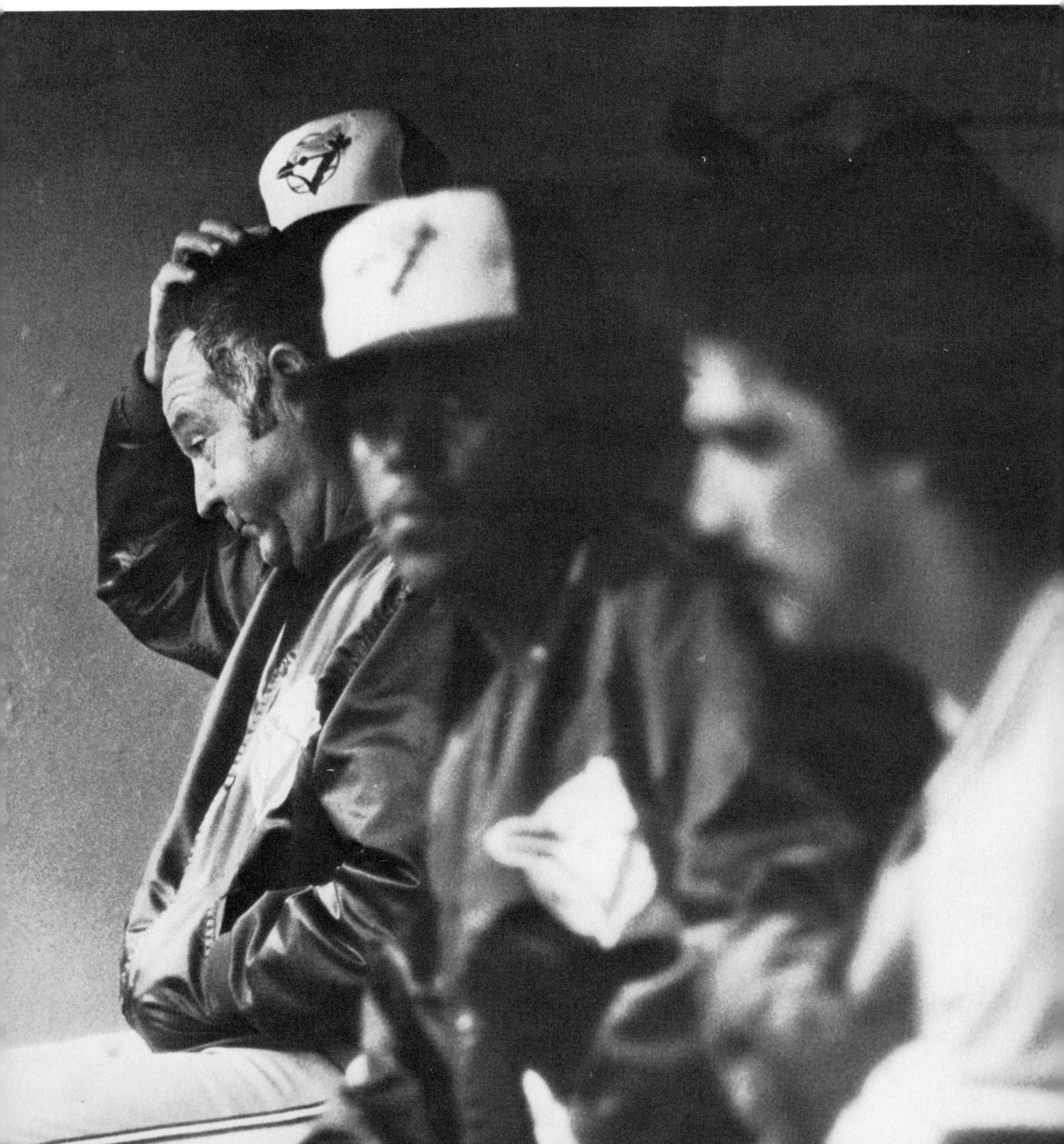

On the first day of spring training in 1977, Bavasi handed out instructions to the team about signing autographs ... about tipping their hats to the crowd when they were applauded ... about keeping their uniforms and travel clothes neat, clean and freshly ironed ... and about staying clean-shaven — no moustaches, beards or long sideburns.

The image of the Blue Jays was set. Toronto was one big, happy, squeaky-clean, baseball family.

The First Toronto Roster Takes Shape

On October 22, 1976, the Jays bought catcher Phil Roof from the Chicago White Sox. Roof became the first player to pull on a Toronto uniform.

Then, on November 5, the American League held an expansion draft. Each established A.L. team got to protect most of its best players from the draft. The Blue Jays and the Seattle Mariners picked for the rest.

Toronto's first pick was Bob Bailor, a versatile fielder with the Baltimore Orioles. Bailor would become the first favorite of the Blue Jays fans.

Some of the original Jays picks didn't even make the club the first year. Others lasted only one season. Still others served the Jays for several seasons. And a very special few were still with the team in the 1980's.

Pitcher Jerry Garvin came from the Minnesota Twins. He won one game as a starter for Toronto in 1977. An arm injury kept him out for most of the 1979 season, but he returned in 1980 as a relief pitcher and picked up eight saves.

1977
The Blue Jays complete their first season with 54 victories and a seventh-place finish with Manager Roy Hartsfield at the helm.

PHOTO
Manager Roy Hartsfield scratches his head after the last inning of a 1979 loss to the powerful Yankees.

13

1977
Outfielder Ron Fairly is picked as Toronto's first All-Star player.

Garvin's right-handed sidekick — Jim Clancy — came from the Texas Rangers. He collected 10 wins in 1978 but was slowed by foot injuries in '79. He rebounded to win 13 games in 1980.

Hard-hitting outfielder Al Woods came from the Twins. In his first major league at-bat, he hit a home run. In his first at-bat as a pinch-hitter, he hit another four-bagger. That tied two big-league records.

Catcher Ernie Whitt came from the Boston Red Sox. Infielders Garth Iorg and Otto Velez both came from the New York Yankees.

As the first-year team took shape, Bavasi and Manager Roy Hartsfield filled in the holes with some clever trades.

On November 5, Toronto got catcher Alan Ashby and first baseman-outfielder Doug Howard from the Cleveland Indians, in return for pitcher Al Fitzmorris.

One month later, Cleveland catcher Rick Cerone and outfielder Jon Lowenstein moved to Toronto, in exchange for first baseman Rico Carty.

Lowenstein barely got settled when he was shipped back to the Indians, this time for infielder Hector Torres.

And so went the juggling of players, the trading and re-trading.

Like a complicated chess match, the Toronto front office had to think three or four deals ahead.

For example, who would have suspected in 1976, that pitcher Pete Vuckovich would eventually help the Jays get two of Toronto's key players six years later? Here's what happened:

1. Vuckvoich was an expansion draft choice from the White Sox.

PHOTO
High-kicker. Jerry Garvin sparkled in this 14-inning marathon win against the Brewers. (1981)

14

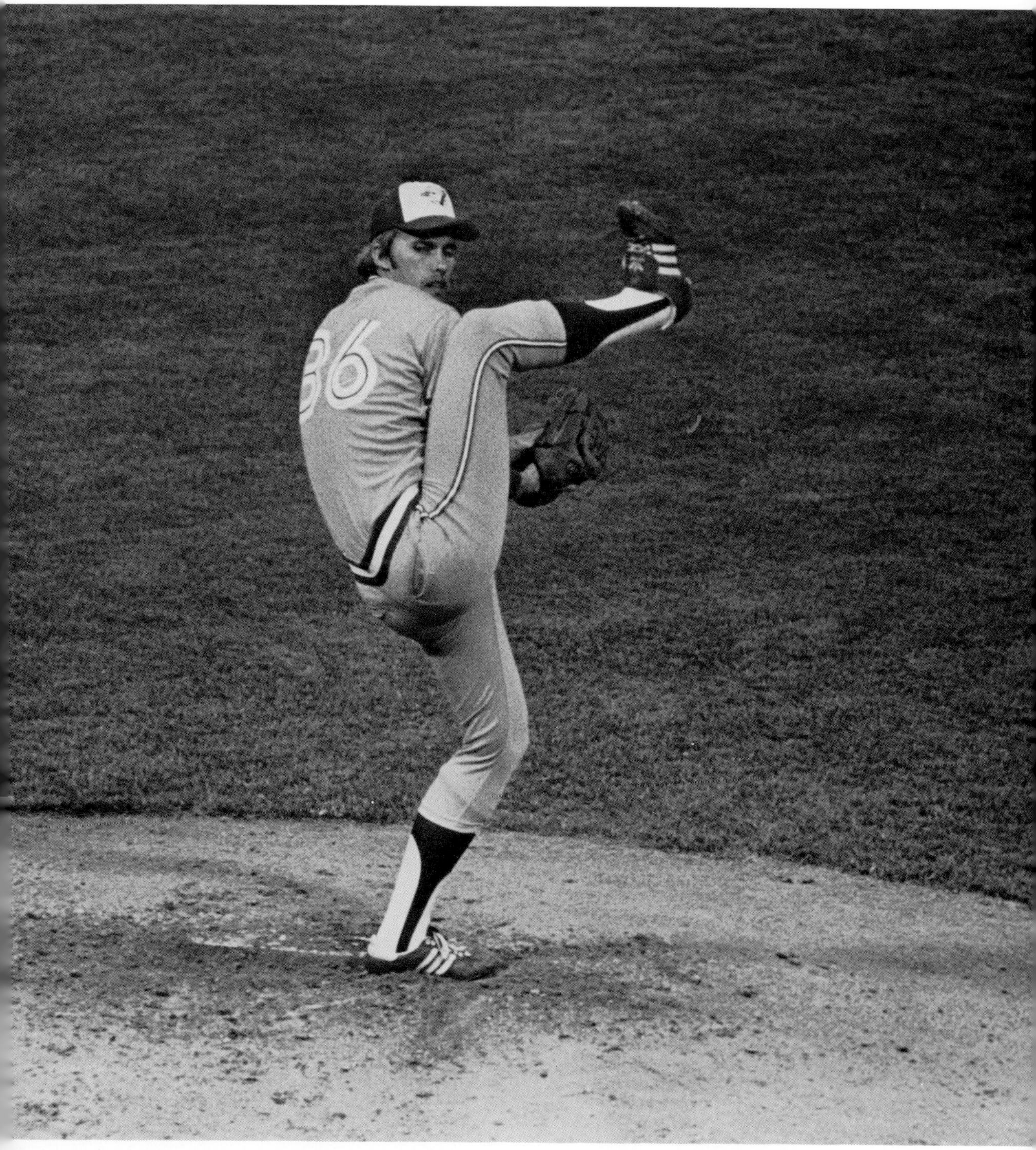

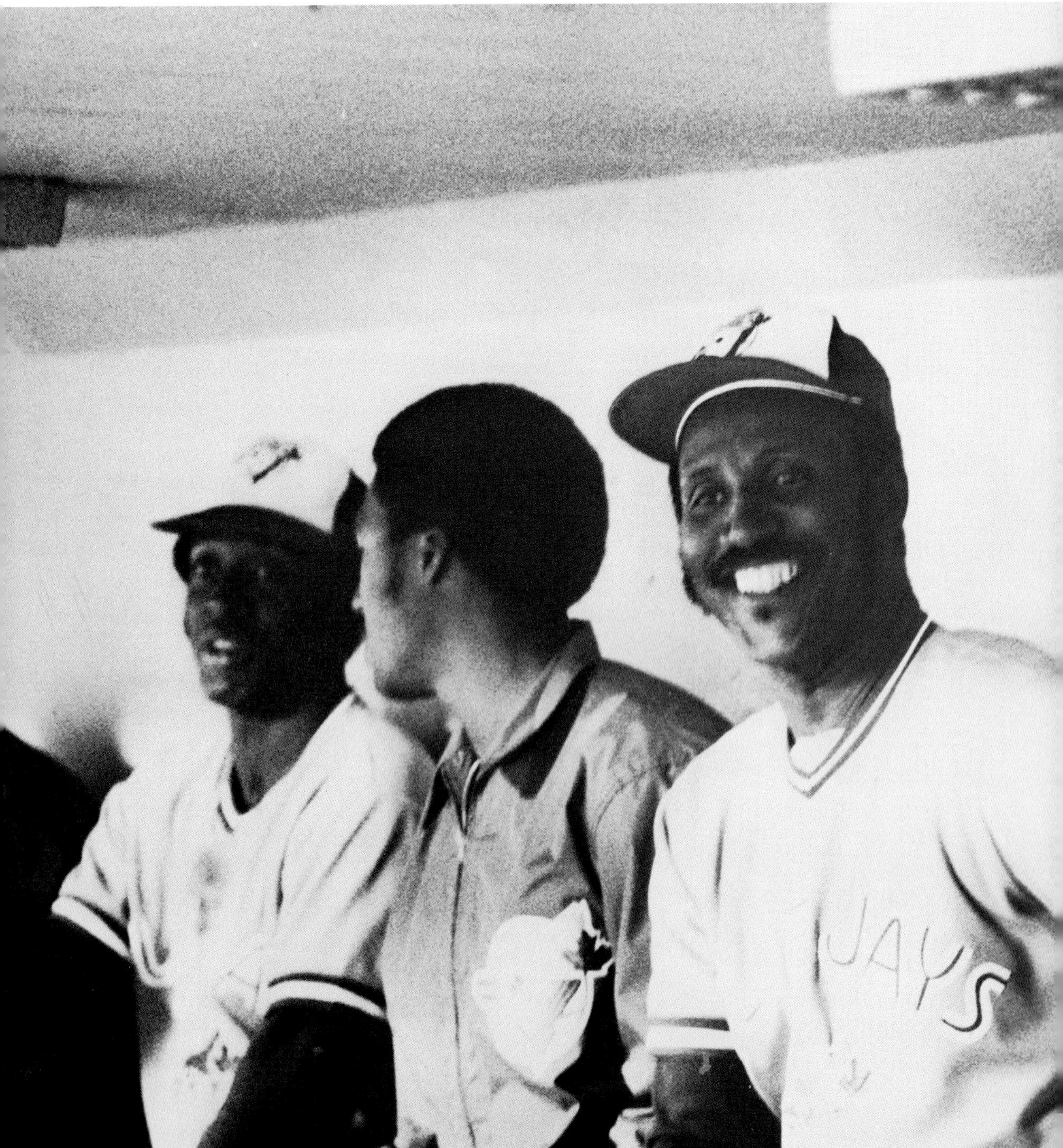
JAYS

2. He was part of a four-player trade in late 1977 that brought southpaw Tom Underwood and righty Victor Cruz to Toronto.

3. In late 1979, Underwood was part of another deal. He went to the Yankees. Chris Chambliss, Paul Mirabella and Damaso Garcia came to the Jays.

4. A month later, Chambliss and Luis Gomez went to Atlanta. Outfielder Barry Bonnell and pitcher Joey McLaughlin, who became Blue Jays in that deal, were still regulars in 1982—thirteen players, four deals and four teams later!

That was the sort of wheeling and dealing that was going on behind the scenes as the Blue Jays began their first training camp in sunny Dunedin, Florida, in the spring of 1977.

The choice of Dunedin was a bit of a relief. It can get mighty cold in Toronto during the winter. In fact, the Blue Jays' fans were already betting that Toronto's home opener April 17 against the White Sox would be "snowed out."

The Blue Jays not only won their first spring training game, 3-1, against the Mets, but they came back to Toronto for their Opening Day and stunned the veteran White Sox.

First baseman Doug Ault became the first hero in Toronto's new Exhibition Stadium. He hit two home runs to ignite the Jays to a 9-5 win. The fans were ecstatic. Major League baseball had officially arrived in Toronto!

The fans played a big part in that first win. Nearly 45,000 Torontonians bundled up on the morning of April 17 and filed into Exhibition Stadium. The pessimists were almost right. It was cold and snowy, well

**1977
Toronto rookie Bob Bailor posts a .310 season batting average—a record for players on first-year expansion clubs.**

**PHOTO
Rico Carty is all smiles after hitting a grand slam homer in the 5th against the Indians.
(1979)**

17

1978
Toronto outfielder Rick Bosetti is named to two All-Rookie teams; Roy Howell is elected to represent Toronto in the annual All-Star Game.

below freezing, but still the fans came. Still the game went on. And still, the Blue Jays won.

If the storybook beginning for the Toronto club would have continued in fairy-tale fashion, the Blue Jays would have kept on winning. They would have challenged for the American League Eastern Division title, maybe even the pennant. With a little luck, they might have even made it into the World Series.

It didn't happen that way, of course. Like every young expansion club, Toronto struggled through the 1977 season. Lineups were juggled and new players were tested. The young players on the club needed time to stretch their wings and grow together. As Peter Bavasi had said, it took patience. There were many bright spots, however.

• Fielder Otto Velez was named American League player of the month in April. During those 30 days, he hit five home runs, drove in 11 runs and scored 11 runs. He led the A.L. in slugging percentage that month at .865, and averaged .422 batting.

• On September 12, Roy Howell sent nine of his teammates home with five hits—two home runs, two doubles and a single. The Jays won, 19-3. Their opponent? The powerful New York Yankees. Toronto's 19 runs turned out to be the most scored against New York in Yankee Stadium in more than 50 years!

• Outfielder Ron Fairly was picked as Toronto's All-Star game representative.

• Bob Bailor at shortstop, Doug Ault at first base and Jerry Garvin on the mound were named to All-Rookie teams.

• On August 9, Toronto beat Minnesota, 6-2, in front of 23,450 Exhibition Stadium fans. That pushed home attendance figures to 1,219,551 after only 50 home games, a new record for a first-year expansion club.

When the turnstiles had clicked for the final time in 1977, more than 1.7 million Blue Jays fans had watched their team perform in Toronto. They paid $8 million for tickets, and another $10 million for Blue Jays souvenirs. Christmas shoppers in 1977 made Blue Jays memorabilia some of the most popular gift items. T-shirts, toys, hats, pennants, decals—you name it, and you could probably buy one in Toronto colors, with the Blue Jays logo.

The final tally showed an estimated $2 million profit for Blue Jays' owners.

A profit! In their first year! With a losing team! No one had heard of such a thing in the history of baseball.

But the city and fans of Toronto were something special. They had shown in the past, with the Maple Leafs and the Argonauts, that they'd support their teams, win or lose. That support meant a lot to the Blue Jays. It would be tested, again and again, over the next few years.

**1979
Alfredo Griffin
is named A.L. Rookie
of the Year.**

Second-Year Squabbles

Like all families, the club had a few difficulties to work out. Oddly enough, the early financial success of the team caused some real problems.

At the beginning of the first season, many of the Blue Jays had signed single-season contracts. This meant that they could try to make a new deal with the owners for the second season.

Several Blue Jays went to Peter Bavasi to renegotiate their contracts. They knew that Toronto had made a profit that year, but they couldn't get the raises they

19

**1980
Bobby Mattick, a former shortstop with the Cubs and Reds, takes over as manager. Toronto records its first winning Exhibition Season.**

wanted.

The average Blue Jays player made $34,300 per year. That sounds like a lot, but the average major league player earned $76,300, and the average Philadelphia Phillies player made $139,900.

The young Blue Jays knew they weren't Phillies. But some, like Bailor and Garvin, felt they had earned the right to a raise.

What the players didn't know was that over the winter of 1977-78, the club had established a $2-million fund. It would be used exclusively to buy new, young players.

By spring training of 1978, veterans Bailor and Garvin were still negotiating. Garvin would end up having his old contract renewed at less than half of the $80,000 he wanted. Bailor did get a new pact, however, at about $80,000.

Like all good players, most of the Blue Jays put aside their differences with Toronto's front office and just tried to play their best for manager Hartsfield when the '78 season began.

Yet, for whatever reasons, Toronto's won-lost record barely improved in 1978, to 59-102. It actually dropped in 1979, to 53-109. Both years, the Blue Jays again finished in the A.L. Eastern Division cellar.

Still, there were silver linings in the clouds over Exhibition Stadium.

• Outfielder Rick Bosetti was named to two all-rookie teams in 1978, as were shortstop Alfredo Griffin and second baseman Danny Ainge in '79.

• In 1978, third baseman Roy Howell represented the team at the All-star game. The next year, manager Roy Hartsfield helped coach the A.L. club, and pitcher Dave Lemanczyk was named an All-Star.

**PHOTO
Toronto hustle. Shortstop Alfredo Griffin went all the way into left field for this fly ball. (1982)**

20

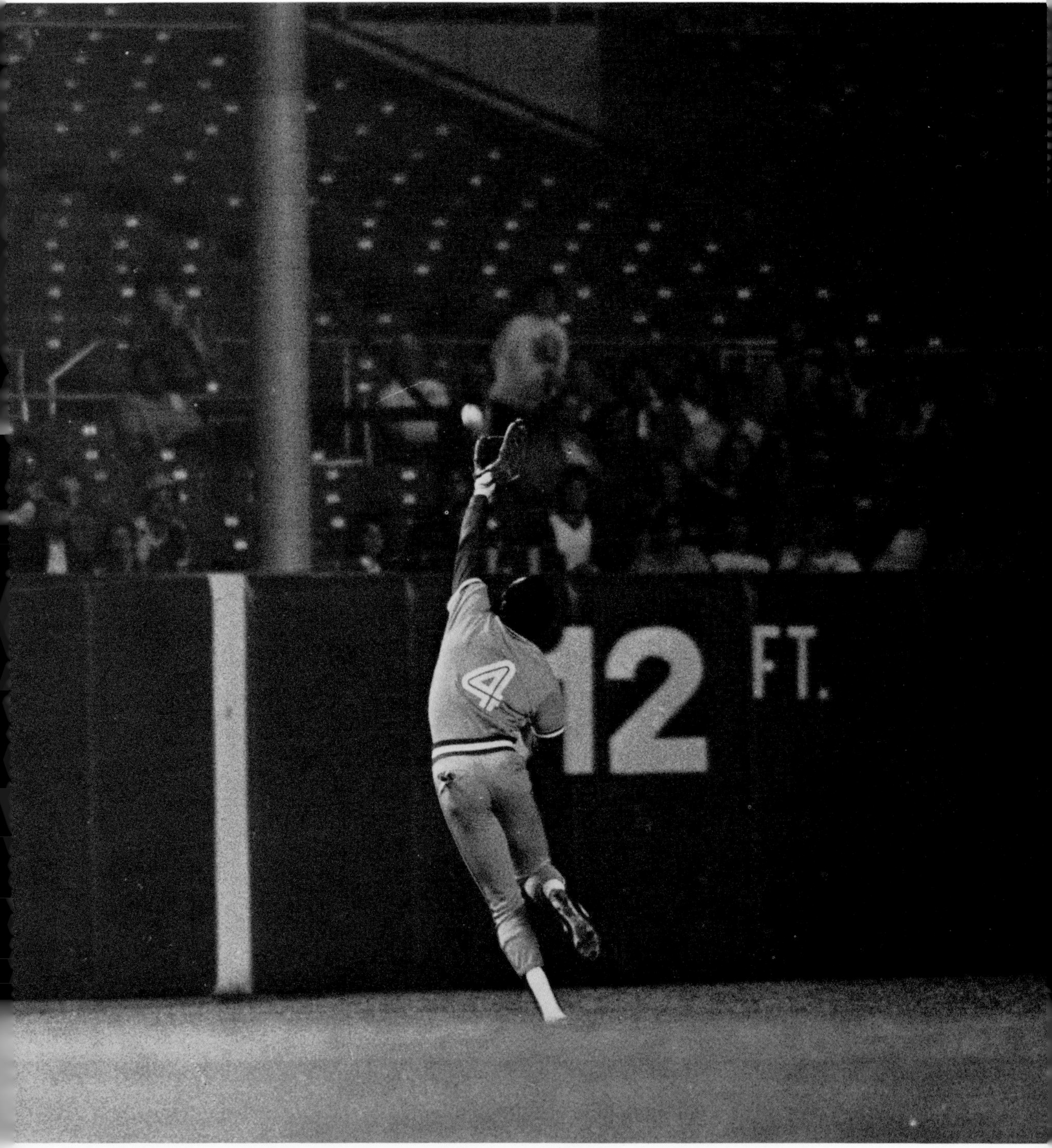
12 FT.

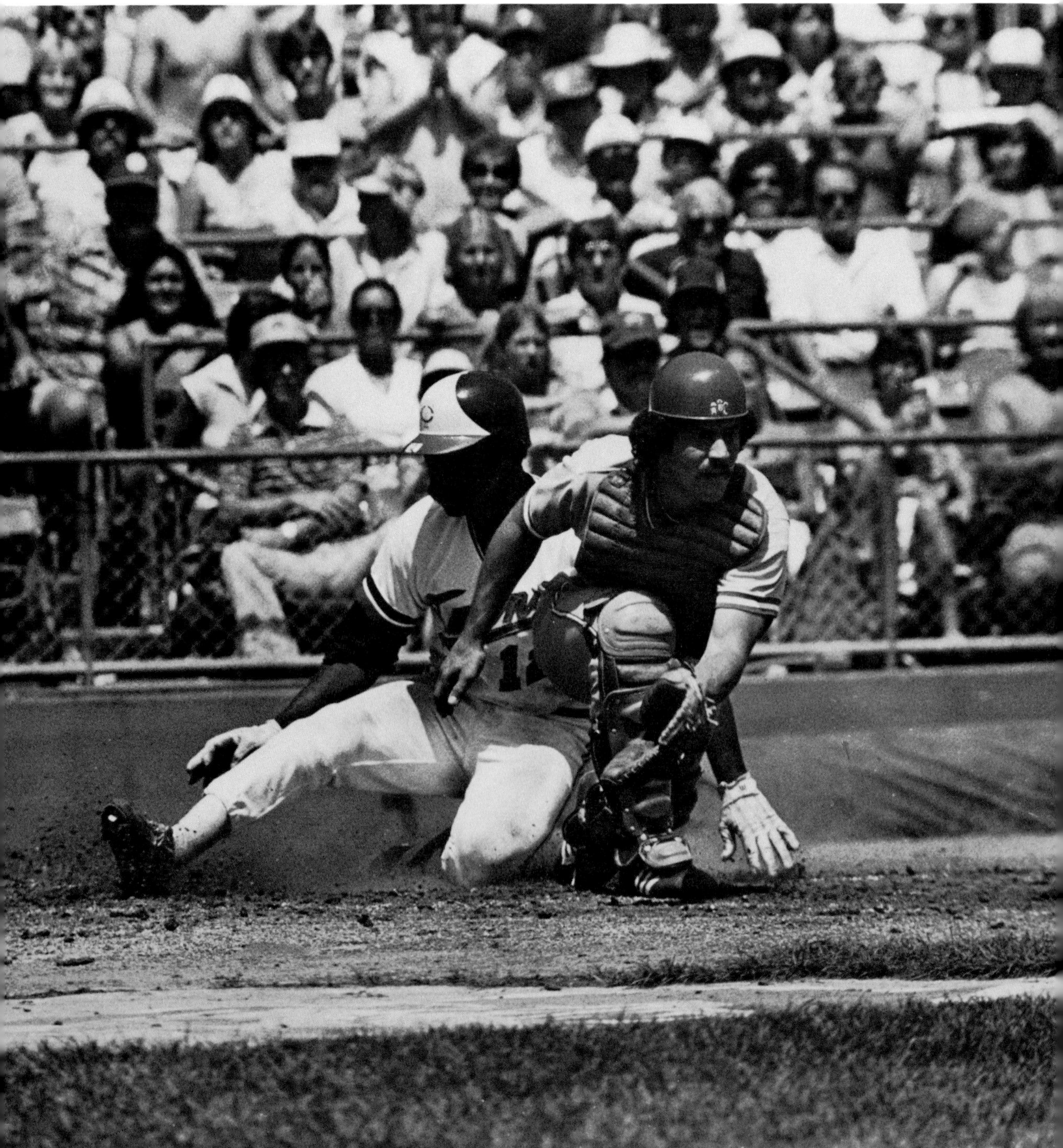

• In 1979, Otto Velez was named A.L. player of the week and Griffin player of the month.

• Griffin set club records in hits (179), runs (81), triples (10) and stolen bases (21). His batting average of .279 was the best among all A.L. shortsops. Griffin was named the league's 1979 Rookie-of-the-Year.

Even with all those positive signs the Blue Jays just couldn't pull themselves out of their doldrums. By the end of the 1979 season, an expansion record total of 4,695,288 fans had seen Toronto play out its first three years. But the Blue Jays' record was second only to the infamous New York Mets as the worst start in the history of major league expansion.

As Bavasi would later admit, "About in the middle of the '79 season, the club spirit began to deteriorate. The players were discouraged. Their confidence was shattered." The Blue Jays were in need of a change.

The Turnaround Begins With Bobby Mattick (1980)

On October 18, 1979, Toronto hired Robert James "Bobby" Mattick as field manager. Now, the tide was about to turn.

Mattick had joined the Blue Jays' organization back in 1976, as a scouting supervisor. He had helped the club draft its original roster. Since then, he had spent his time either signing, scouting for trades or developing practically every top young Toronto player.

Needless to say, Mattick was very highly respected in Toronto. But when Bavasi came to him and asked him to become manager, Mattick said no.

Bavasi asked again. Mattick said no again.

Finally, on Bavasi's third try, Mattick agreed. "If

**Oct. 4, 1980
Toronto defeats the BoSox, 7-6, in a 17-inning marathon.**

**PHOTO
Jays' catcher Rick Cerone slammed lots of doors before the Yankees bought his services in the '80s.**

**1982
Jesse Barfield
launches 22 homers,
an all-time club
record for a rookie.**

you've got enough guts to ask me, I guess I've got enough guts to try it," Mattick said.

You see, Mattick wasn't your run-of-the-mill manager. At 64, he had many years of experience as a scout, but he had never been a major league manager before.

So Toronto got itself a 64-year-old rookie manager, and Bavasi couldn't have been happier.

"Bobby's just what we needed," said Bavasi, who was now the Blue Jays' President. "He relates to young players and has been one of the architects of our long-range plans. Plus, he was involved in the development of the Milwaukee and Montreal clubs into contenders."

Mattick carried his age well. He had a full head of hair, a smiling face and a positive outlook on life. He was the ultimate optimist, with enough realism thrown in to keep faith with his players. He had a good sense of humor, and won over the press by cordially inviting them to share a post-game beer. He knew each of the Blue Jays personally, and he knew what was needed to get the club on the winning trail.

Still, he was set apart from other managers. He was rusty in giving signs to his batters, but he practiced for hours in front of a mirror. He had to be talked into pulling on the Toronto uniform — he wanted to manage in a business suit. He refused to walk to the mound to replace one of his pitchers. He'd send an assistant instead.

"People don't pay good money to come to the game and see an old man running around on the field," Mattick explained.

With Mattick at the helm, the Blue Jays began to improve. The players were happier, now, because their new skipper helped them improve their game, while letting them be their natural selves. "I don't believe in too many rules," he'd say, and before long some of the Blue Jays were sporting longer hair and moustaches.

Toronto recorded its first-ever winning exhibition season in 1980 — coming out on top in 10 of 17 games. Then, in their first two home games, the Blue Jays beat the powerful Milwaukee Brewers, 11-2, then 1-0.

Mattick wasn't the only reason for the turnaround. Alfredo Griffin got better and better at shortstop. Dave Stieb, Paul Mirabella and Jim Clancy anchored an improving pitching staff. Rookie second baseman Damaso Garcia began to show the talent that would earn him spots on two All-Rookie teams. Meanwhile, the rest of the Blue Jays got caught up in that winning feeling, too.

April of 1980 went down in Blue Jays' history as the first month that the club put it all together.

• They won 9 games and lost 7, a .563 winning percentage.

• They recorded a 3.26 earned run average, lowest ever for Toronto pitchers.

• They beat the Brewers five straight games.

• Stieb won all three of his games in April and was named American League pitcher of the month.

• And, best of all, Toronto passed the Yankees, the Red Sox, the Brewers and the Orioles, and sat proudly in first place of the Eastern Division.

Remember, though, that a baseball season is 162 games long. The great start, glorious as it was, began to fade as the summer months approached.

Toronto's won-lost record kept dropping as each month passed. The Jays went 13-14 in May... 10-17 in June... 11-17 in July... 11-20 in August... and 13-20 in the final two months.

1982 Toronto ace Dave Stieb sets a new club record with 17 victories for the season.

PHOTO SPREAD NEXT PAGE Jesse Barfield swings for the fences in '86. Barfield exploded for 40 homers that year.

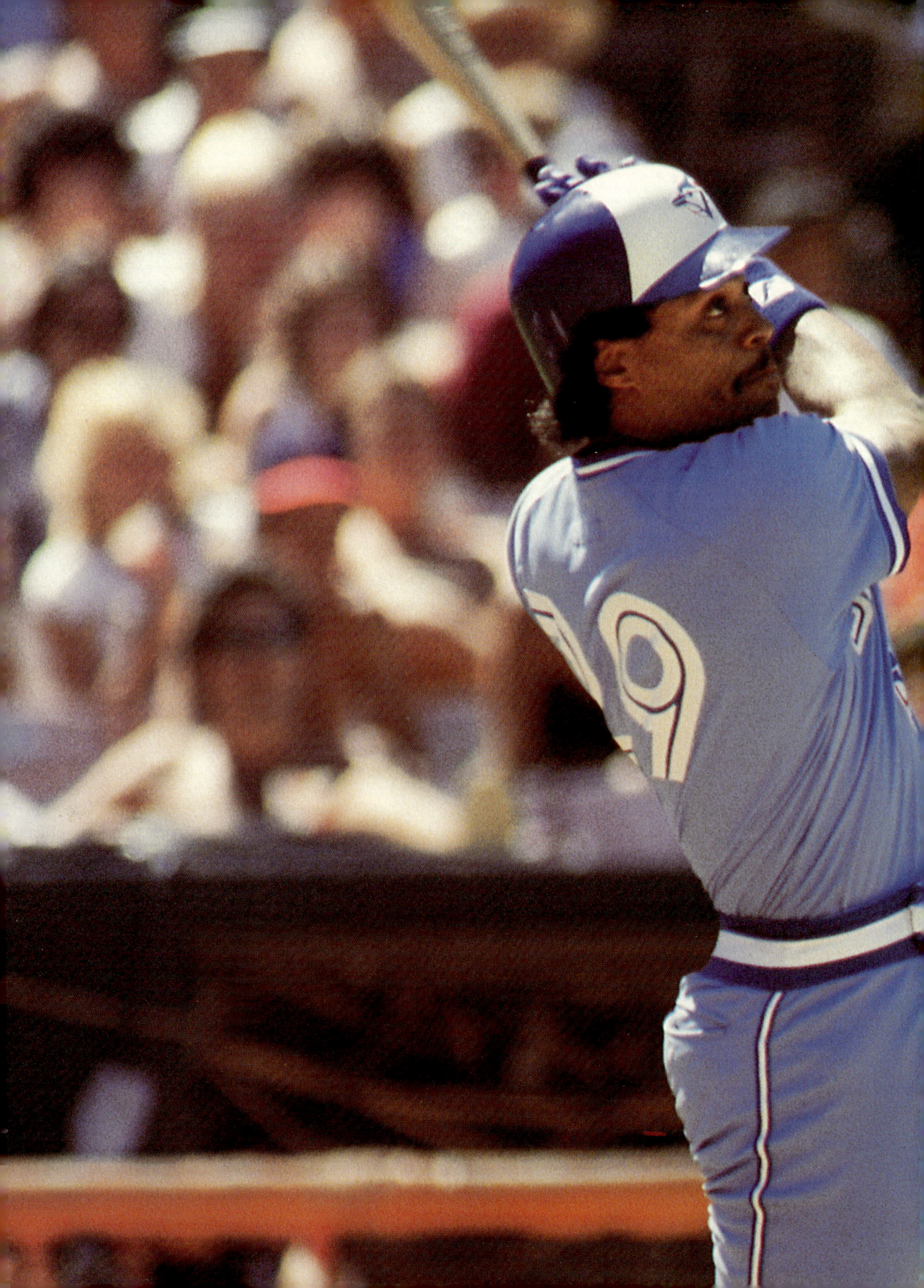

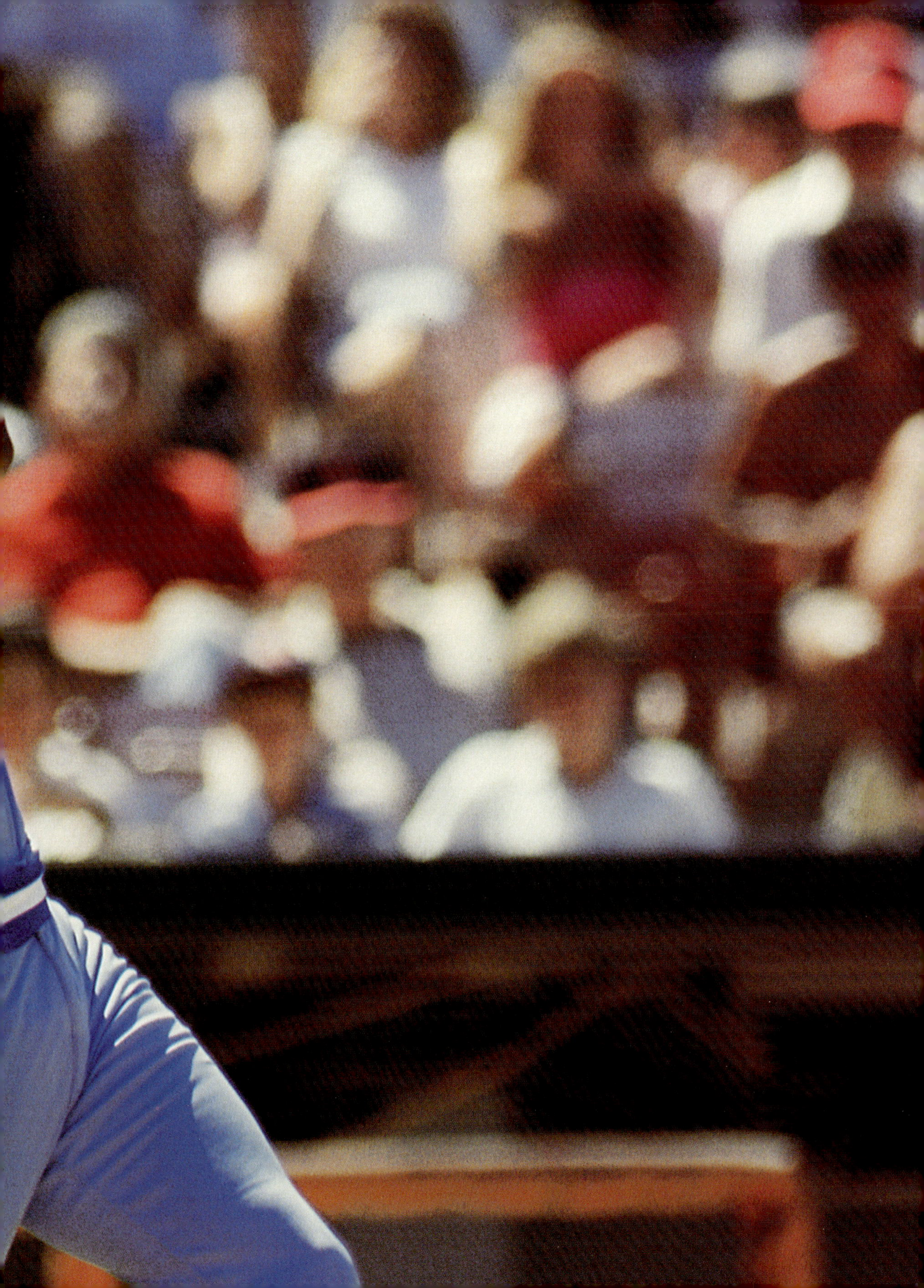

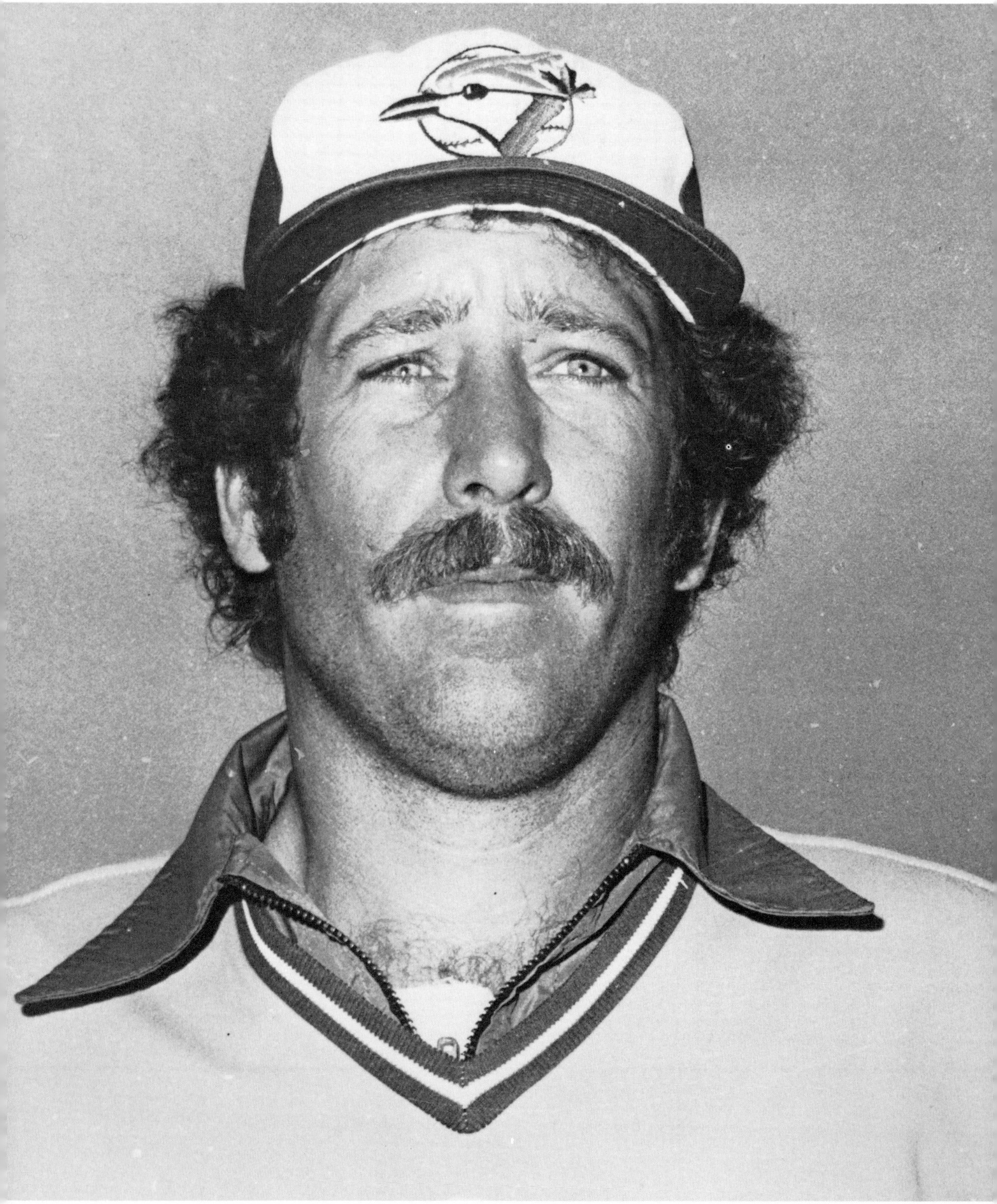

Still, a milestone had been reached. Toronto had won 67 games in 1980, and lost 95 — their fewest ever. Though they still finished last in their division, their winning percentage had hopped to .414.

The momentum from 1980 carried over to 1981 in a negative way. The Blue Jays got a slow start, winning only 7 of 19 games in April; 9 of 29 in May; 0 of 10 in June.

Then a league-wide players' strike was called. Toronto missed 55 games because of it. But when the Jays got going again after the walkout, it was as if 1980 never ended. After winning 16 and losing 42 in the first half of the split season, Toronto won 21 and lost 27 in the second half.

Through the first four weeks of the second half, the Blue Jays were in first, second, third or fourth place in their division. They had a .500 record on September 22, but slipped in the final two weeks to finish at .438.

Still, Toronto had served notice of better things to come. First baseman John Mayberry slugged 17 home runs. In the second half of the season, the club batted .237. The starting pitchers got stronger as the year progressed. And two relief aces, Roy Lee Jackson and Joey McLaughlin, came into their own.

The Blue Jays had to adapt again for the 1982 season when Mattick was promoted to Executive Coordinator of Baseball Operations. His replacement as manager was another former infielder, Robert Joe "Bobby" Cox, a man who was about to lead the Blue Jays higher than they had ever flown before.

**1983
Jesse Barfield sets several club home run records, including a cluster of 10 homers in one month.**

**PHOTO
Mike Willis threw his share of whistlers in 1979.**

1983
The Jays record their first winning A.L. season, their highest finish to that point, and the best attendance record in club history.

PHOTO
Gotcha! Toronto's Rance Mullinic with one of his patented shoestring grabs. (1986)

Bobby Cox Begins His Magic Act (1982)

He was like a magician pulling rabbits out of a hat. Each time the 1982 Blue Jays looked as if they were about to come up empty-handed losers, their crafty new manager would reach down and come up with a new trick.

Bobby Cox started out by telling the players that he intended to "platoon" them, meaning that several different players might rotate at the same position. Or, in some cases, one player might be rotated from one position to another, depending on the Blue Jays' opponent for a particular day.

If the Jays were facing a team of long-ball hitters like the Yankees, Cox placed his fastest players in the outfield. If, on the other hand, Toronto was going against a run-and-gun team like the Cardinals, Cox might position his speed in the infield.

Cox had a knack for reaching into the dugout for the right pinch-hitter, too. By season's end, Toronto had tied the league record for pinch-hitting with 71 hits and 53 runs, many of them game-winners.

"To be honest," said power-hitting second baseman Damaso Garcia, "the players never knew from game to game what Bobby would do next. It kept us on our toes."

It kept the Toronto fans on the edge of their seats, too. More than 1.2 million spectators flocked to Exhibition Stadium that year to watch Bobby and the Blue Jays work their magic. No, Toronto didn't win the Division Championship in '82, but they *did* set a promising new standard of excellence in several departments.

For starters, the Jays recorded their very first winning

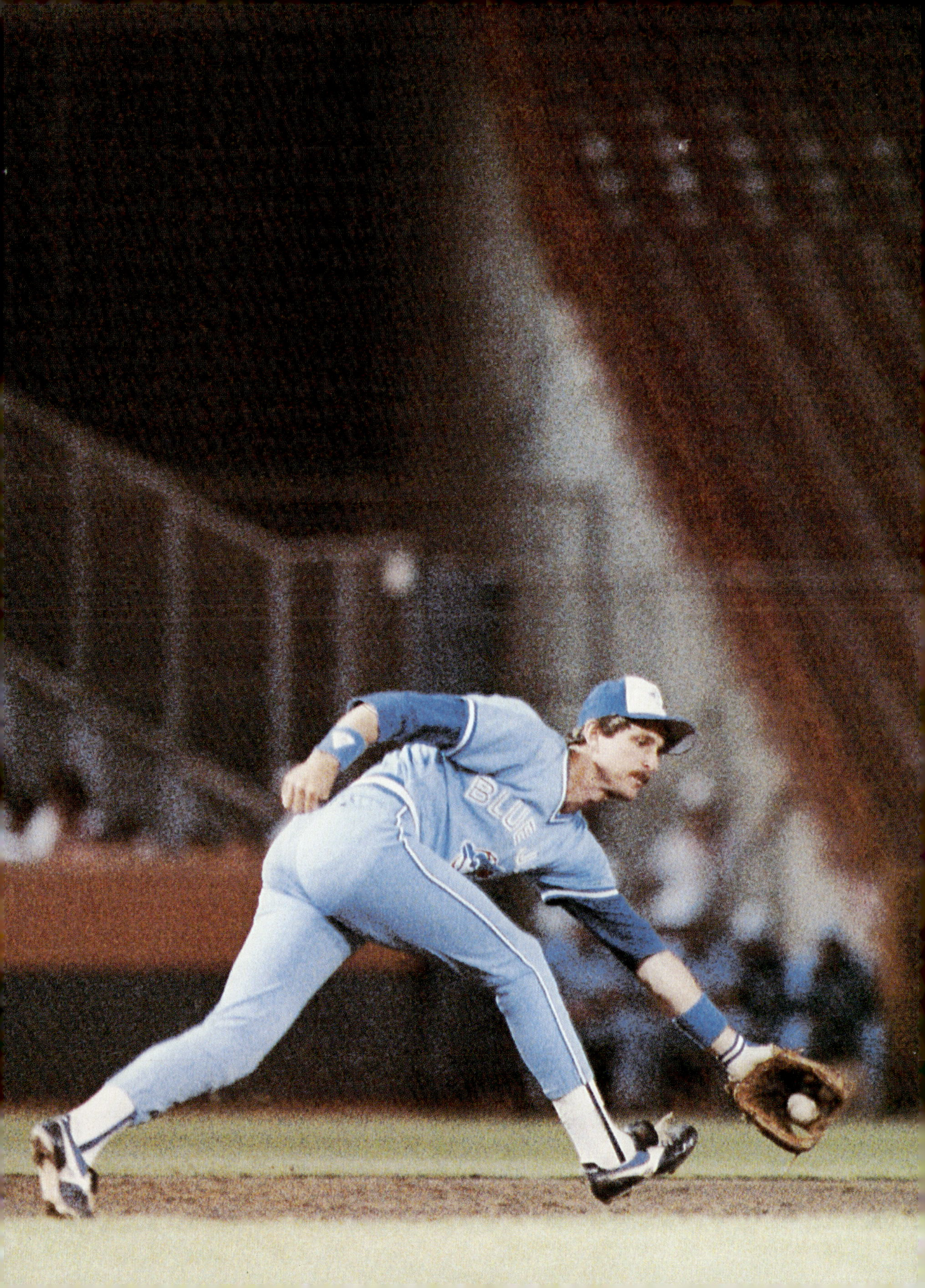
BLUE

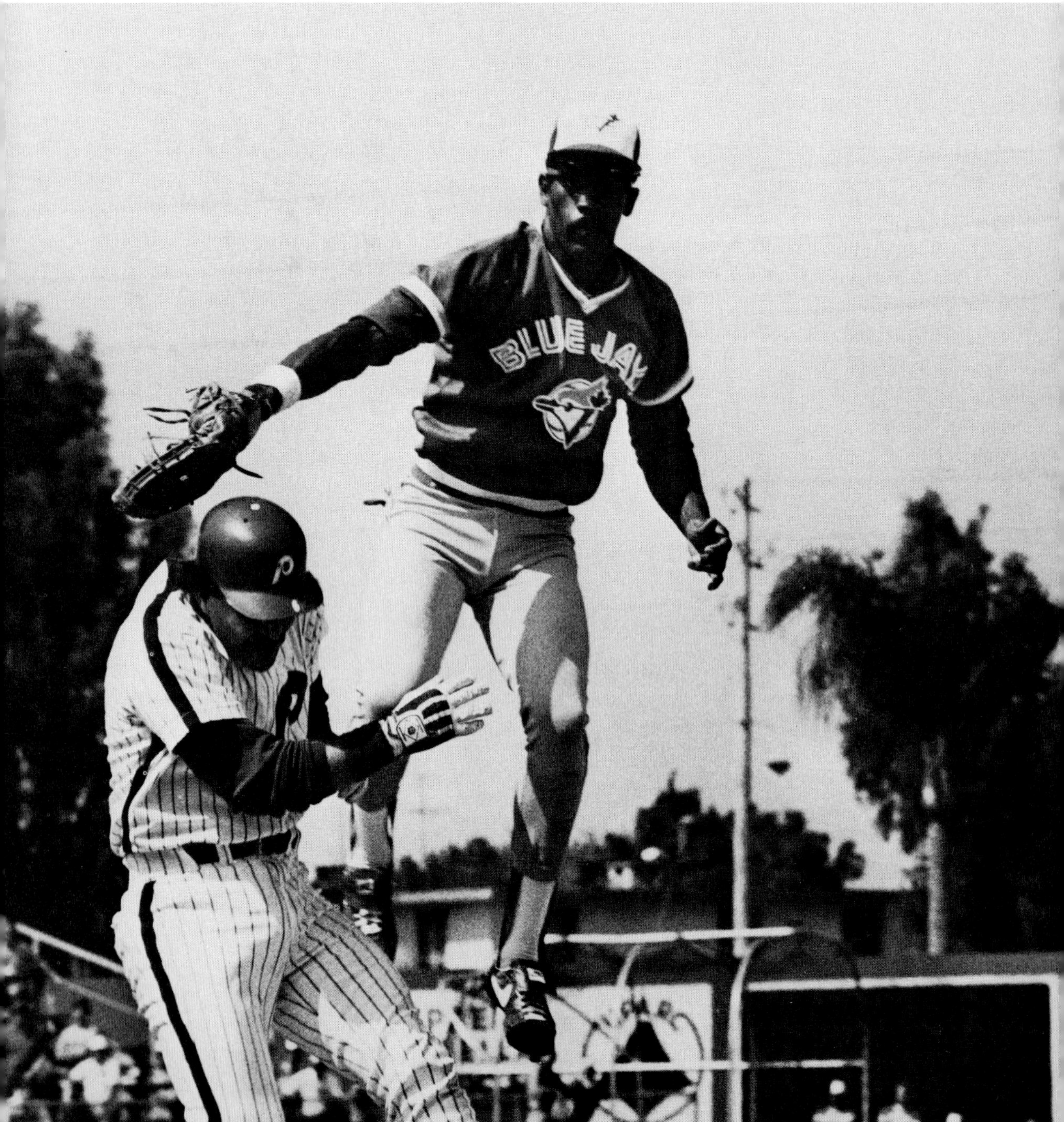

record (44-37) at home that year to the delight of those bigger/better home-town crowds.

While playing on his toes, Garcia led the club with a .310 batting average and set new Toronto records in hits (185), runs scored (89) and pilfered bases (54).

Willie Upshaw's bat came alive for 21 homers, 75 RBIs and a team-record 14 game-winning hits!

Rookie outfielder Jesse "Bazooka" Barfield hurled a few bombs from the fence in '82 that sailed all the way to home plate for picture-perfect tags.

Meanwhile, three starting pitchers — Dave Stieb, Jim Clancy and Luis Leal — threw fewer walks than any other three starters in the league. And let's not forget "Mr. Consistent" — shortstop Alfredo Griffin — who played in all 162 games and committed just seven errors over the entire summer!

It all added up to the finest season in Blue Jay history. Bobby Cox and his boys finished with a respectable 78-84 record, a mere one game behind the same New York Yankee team that had been champs of the American League East just one year earlier.

"Was Cox for real?" wondered the fans. "Did he do it all with mirrors? Could he come back in 1983 and repeat the feat?" Pleasant answers to those questions were just around the bend.

Toronto Power Surge Jolts A.L. East!

Every sport has a special sound. In basketball, it's the crisp "snap" of the twine as an 18-footer hits nothing but net. In football, it's the lone cadence of the quarterback, or the combined snarls of eight angry linemen charging into the pack.

1984 Pitcher Doyle Alexander wins the first of back-to-back 17-victory seasons.

PHOTO Willie Upshaw goes into his high-flying act at first. (1982)

1985
Manager Bobby Cox leads the Jays to their first A.L. Eastern Division championship.

Of all the special sounds of baseball, none is sweeter or more stirring than the sharp, powerful "crack" of hardwood on horsehide. That is the music which the 1983 Toronto Blue Jays played all summer long for their loyal fans in Exhibition Stadium.

Crack! The Jays, led by Willie Upshaw, Jesse Barfield, Cliff Johnson, Lloyd Moseby and Ernie Witt, drilled 101 of the Expos' 167 home runs in their home park that year.

Crack! Toronto hitters were the best unit in the majors with a scintillating .277 average for the season.

Crack! Upshaw batted .306 and set a new Toronto record with 104 RBIs.

Crack! Moseby batted .315, became the first Blue Jay in history to score 100 runs (finishing with 104), and stole 27 bases.

"Awesome Power Carries Blue Jays To League Lead," read a banner headline in a Toronto newspaper in late May. From there, it only got better. For six straight weeks, Toronto's hard-hitting lineup held onto the division lead by demoralizing enemy pitchers with hit after hit, long ball after long ball.

Then, in late August, just when the Toronto fans were getting the hang of chanting, "We're No. 1," a torrent of bad breaks swept the Blue Jays off their perch. A weird seven-game losing streak occurred in which the Jays lost six of the seven in the ninth inning or later. Up to that point, the club had not lost a single extra-inning game all season.

"Every team gets its share of bad breaks," said Manager Cox. "It's just that ours were all clustered together in a one-week stretch. Except for that one bad week, these guys put together a fantastic season. We learned

PHOTO
Lloyd Moseby is headed for home in 1986 game action in Toronto.

34

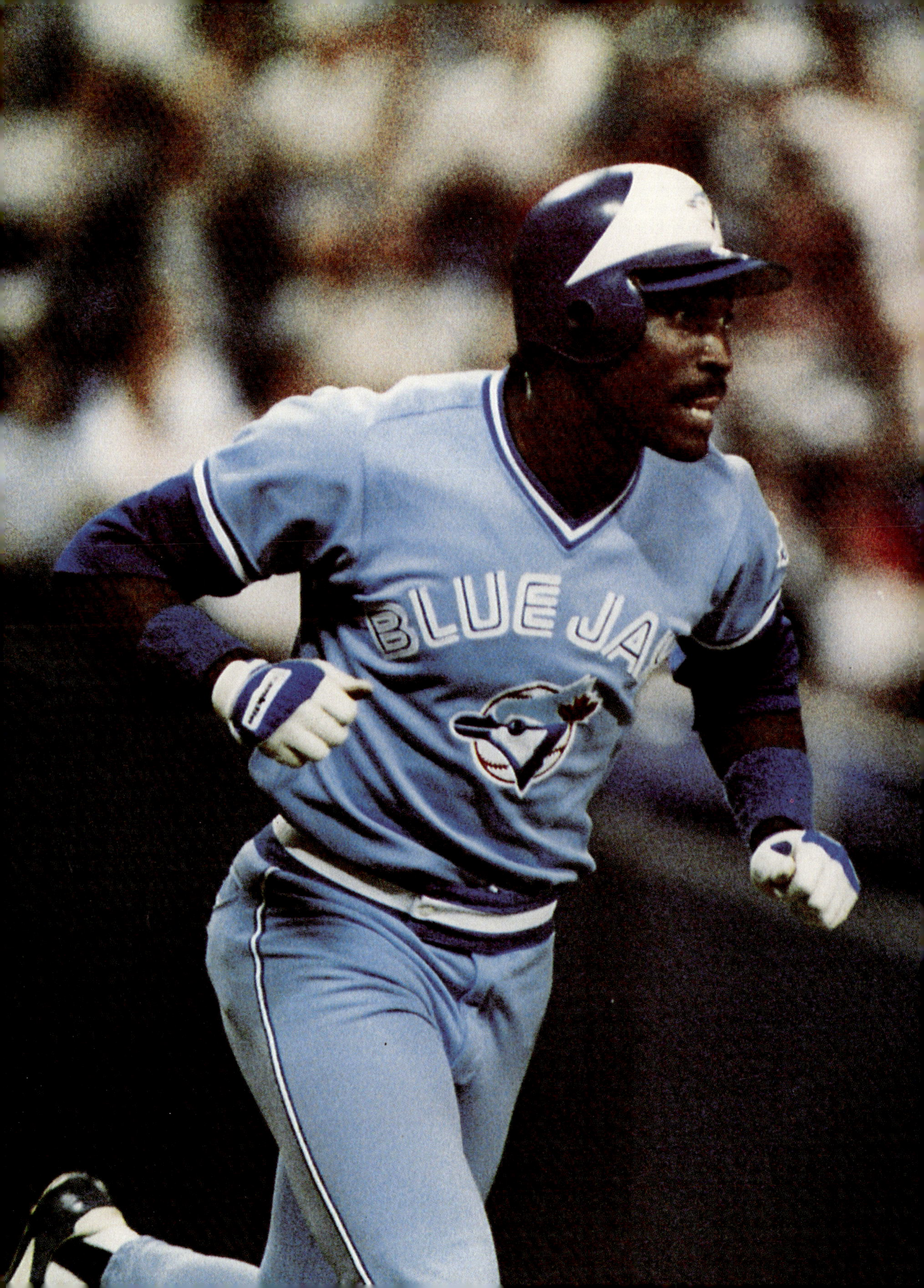
BLUE JA

1985
The Blue Jays set a club record of 13 straight games with one or more home runs, including a five-homer barrage against the Seattle Mariners on July 10.

how to have fun. We learned how to win. And we gave our fans something to cheer about."

In the end, the '83 Jays could point proudly to their first winning A.L. season (89-73), their highest finish (fourth), and a new attendance record of nearly two million fans!

Yup, Bobby Cox was for real.

Jays Glimpse Championship On Horizon

It should've happened in 1984. The Blue Jays, led by ace pitcher Doyle Alexander's 17 victories and George Bell's 87 runs and 26 homers, should've won the Division Championship.

They had the talent and management to do it. They had the necessary desire. They had the vision. They could look out over the rest of the league and see all the way to the championship. Only one obstacle stood in their way out there: The amazing Detroit Tigers.

You see, the Tigers got off to the fastest start in baseball history in 1984, winning 35 of their first 40 games . . . *before* the Blue Jays even had the chance to play them. The Jays did close the gap over the course of the season, and they also had the satisfaction of beating up on the Tigers several times. But they never quite caught them in the standings.

"We did just about everything we set out to do, except win the championship," said a dejected Bobby Cox at season's end. The Tigers were champs that year by a margin of 15 games, but the Blue Jays came in second, their first finish ever in the upper half of the

**PHOTO
Not this time! Fleet-footed Tony Manrique is forced out by Phillies' catcher Ozzie Virgil. (1982)**

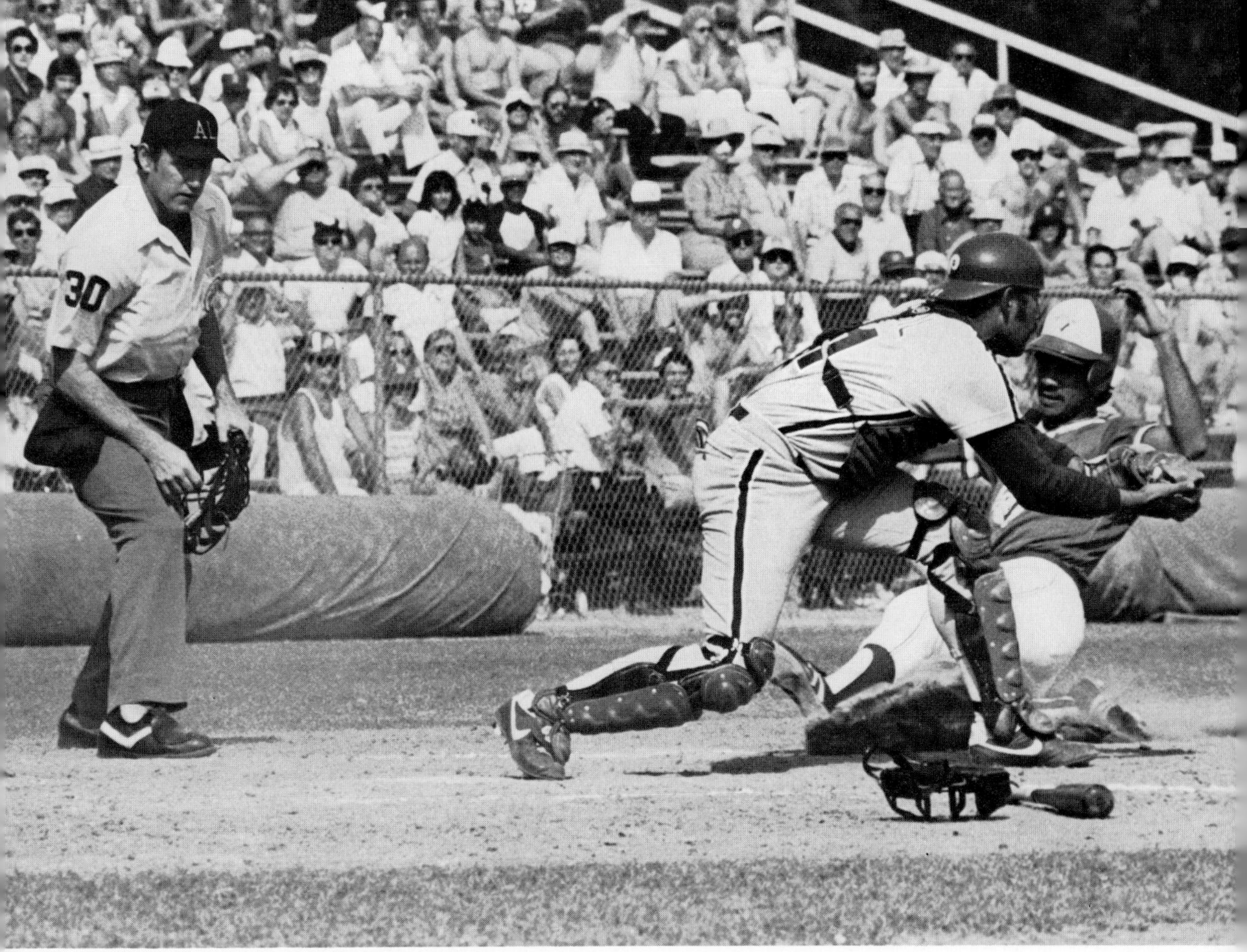
AL
30

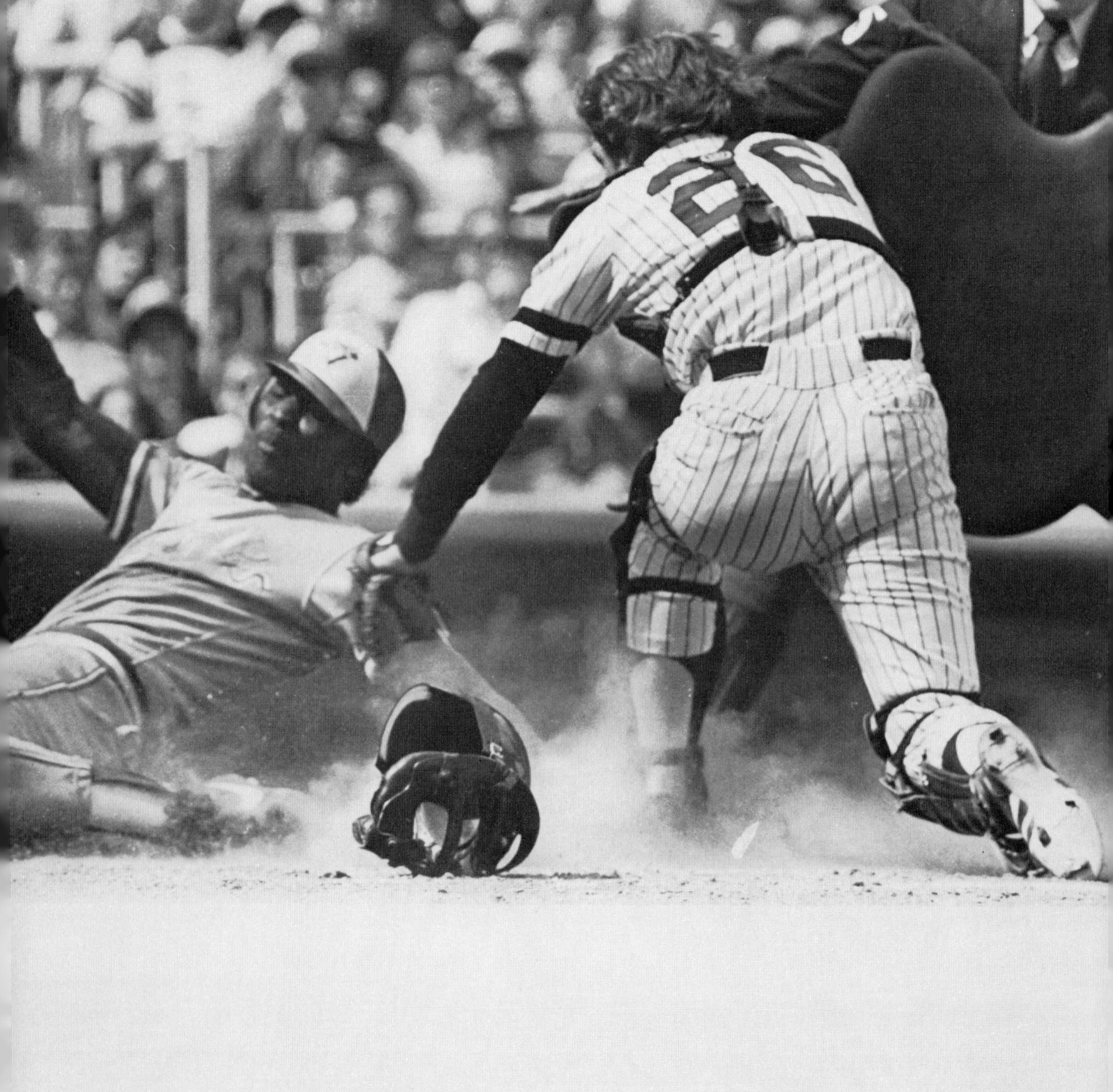

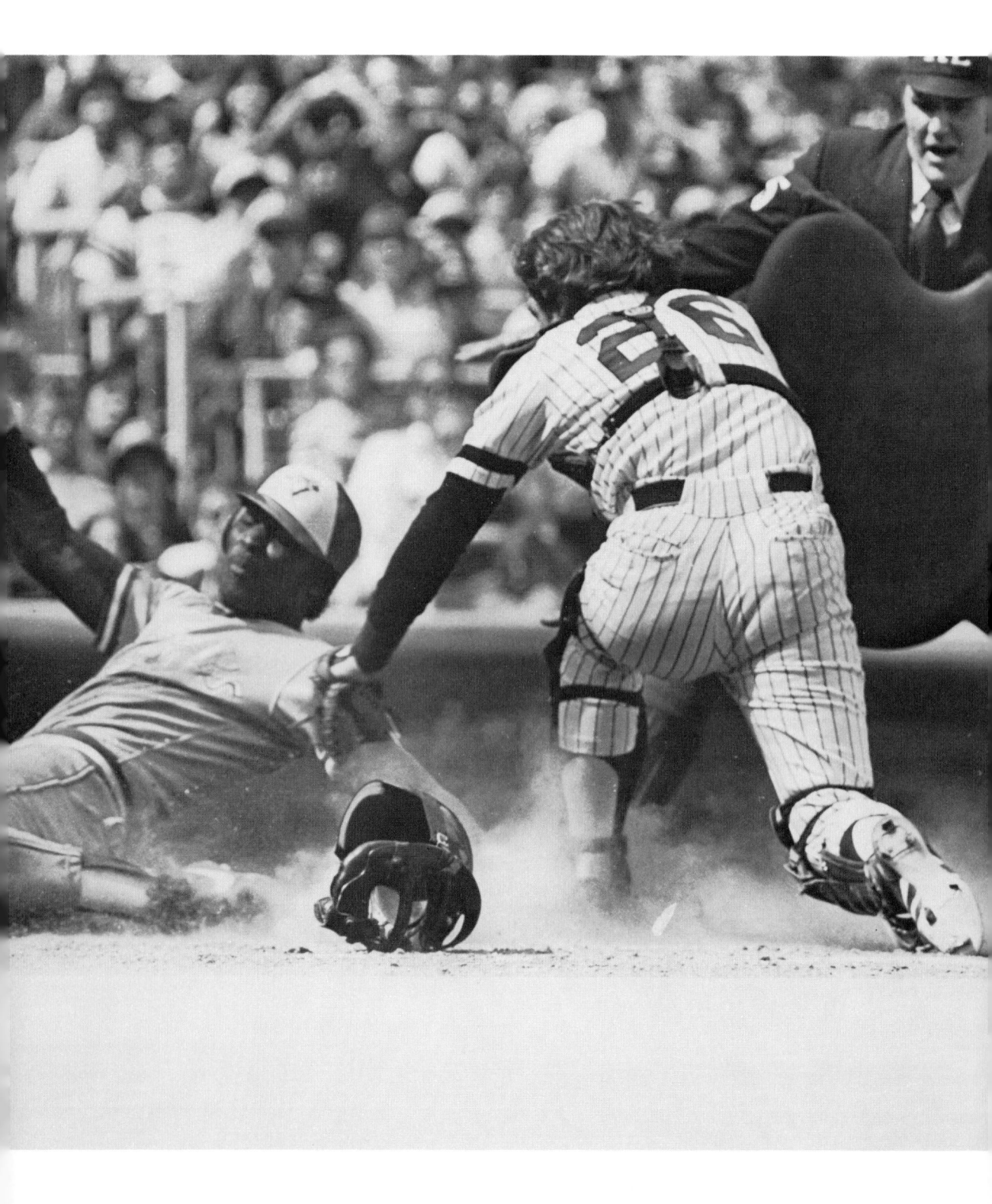

division.

For three consecutive years, Bobby Cox had led his teams closer and closer to the top. It should've happened in 1984. It *did* happen in 1985.

**1985
Bobby Cox
is crowned
The Sporting News'
Major League
Manager of
the Year.**

Champs At Last!

The 1985 campaign was a special one for every baseball fan in Toronto, but especially for sportswriter Neil MacCarl. For years, MacCarl had written about the club's tough times and lowlights. Now, it was his turn to chronicle the good times and the highlights. He put it this way:

"With a team devoid of superstars but loaded with solid players, Manager Bobby Cox led the Toronto Blue Jays to the top of the American League East in the franchise's ninth year of existence.

"Although the Blue Jays ruled the division for 152 (of 182) days in 1985, they still had to fight off a determined late challenge by the New York Yankees to establish their credentials.

"After taking sole possession of first place for good May 20, Toronto finally shut the door October 5 when righthander Doyle Alexander threw a masterful five-hitter. Moseby, catcher Ernie Whitt and first baseman Willie Upshaw hit home runs in a 5-1 victory that climaxed the club's nine-year climb from worst to first."

But there was no time to stop and celebrate. Just ahead was the best-of-seven American League Championship series against the Kansas City Royals and their superstar, George Brett.

Oh, how Cox and the Blue Jays yearned to defeat the Royals. By doing so, Toronto would become the first

**PHOTO
Safe at home!
Lloyd Moseby went
for it all in this
1981 win over
the Yanks.**

39

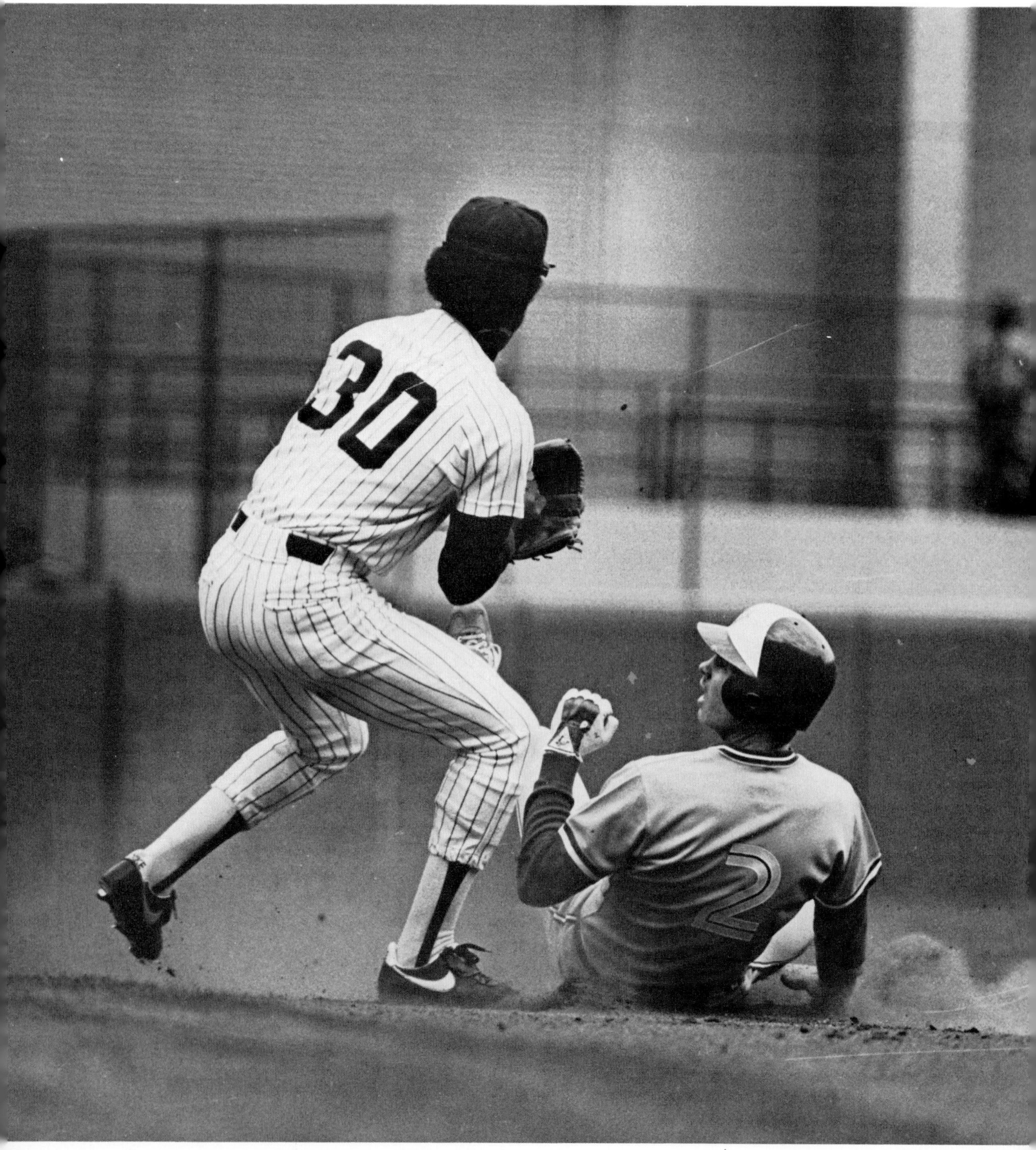
30
2

Canadian team in history to play in the World Series!

With 20 million Canadians glued to their television sets, the Blue Jays jumped out to a big lead, winning three of the first four games. Just one more victory, and the World Series would be theirs. But, it was not to be. The Royals fought back for three straight, and the Blue Jays' beautiful dream sank like the Canadian Sunset in the East.

"We gave it our best shot, I'll say that," shrugged Bobby Cox, but he didn't have to say it. Everyone in Toronto already knew it.

In just four years, Cox had taken the Jays from nowhere to champions of the American League East. Now, he said, it was time for him to move on. When the post-season celebrations died down, Cox was crowned The Sporting News' Major League Manager of the Year. He chose that moment to announce that he was swapping his manager's cap for a shirt and tie. Cox had accepted a front-office job as General Manager of the Atlanta Braves.

So Much Talent!

Following Bobby Cox and taking over a division winner was kind of a no-win situation for new manager Jimy Williams. How could Jimy top Bobby's act? After all, very few teams in the majors had ever been able to win back-to-back division championships, even when the same manager *did* return to lead his club the second year. For a first-year manager to do it in the tough American League East ... well, it was a lot to ask.

All things considered, Jimy did a fine job in 1986. Toronto erupted for more runs (809) and home runs

**1986
Jim Williams takes the manager's reins from Bobby Cox.**

**PHOTO
Did I do it? Danny Ainge steals second in a 2-1 win over the Yanks. (1981)**

41

1986
Jesse Barfield belts 40 homers, an all-time single season record for the Jays.

(181) than they ever had before. In addition, their fielding was Gold Glove quality all the way—only 100 errors, an American League low, for the entire season. The only real disappointment was the pitching, which went from about the best in the league in 1985 to the worst in '86.

Poor Dave Stieb. The big righthander developed bone spurs in his elbow and pitched in pain through most of his starts. He lost the first six, but came on to finish 7-12 for the season. Not bad, but far off the mark from his blistering 17-win record of the year before. Stieb's stablemates—Doyle Alexander and Jimmy Key—also slumped, leaving the Blue Jays all but powerless on the mound.

By season's end, the Jays had toppled from first to fourth. But Pat Gillick, Toronto's highly-respected General Manager, was right there to catch them. Gillick wasted no time.

First, he gave Manager Williams a public vote of confidence, assuring the Toronto fans that the team was in excellent hands.

Next, Gillick got on the telephone and made some crafty moves to strengthen the roster. He would keep the best veterans from the '85 Division Championship team, but he would haul up a few secret weapons from the farm system.

By spring training, 1987, Gillick's weapons were in place. One morning in Dunedin, Florida, a writer for the *Seattle Sports Intelligencer* was watching the Blue Jays work out.

"So...much...talent," he whispered in awe to the reporters on either side of him. "Gillick opens the club-

PHOTO
The ump's-eye view of Toronto pitcher Rusty Stieb pulling the trigger. (1986)

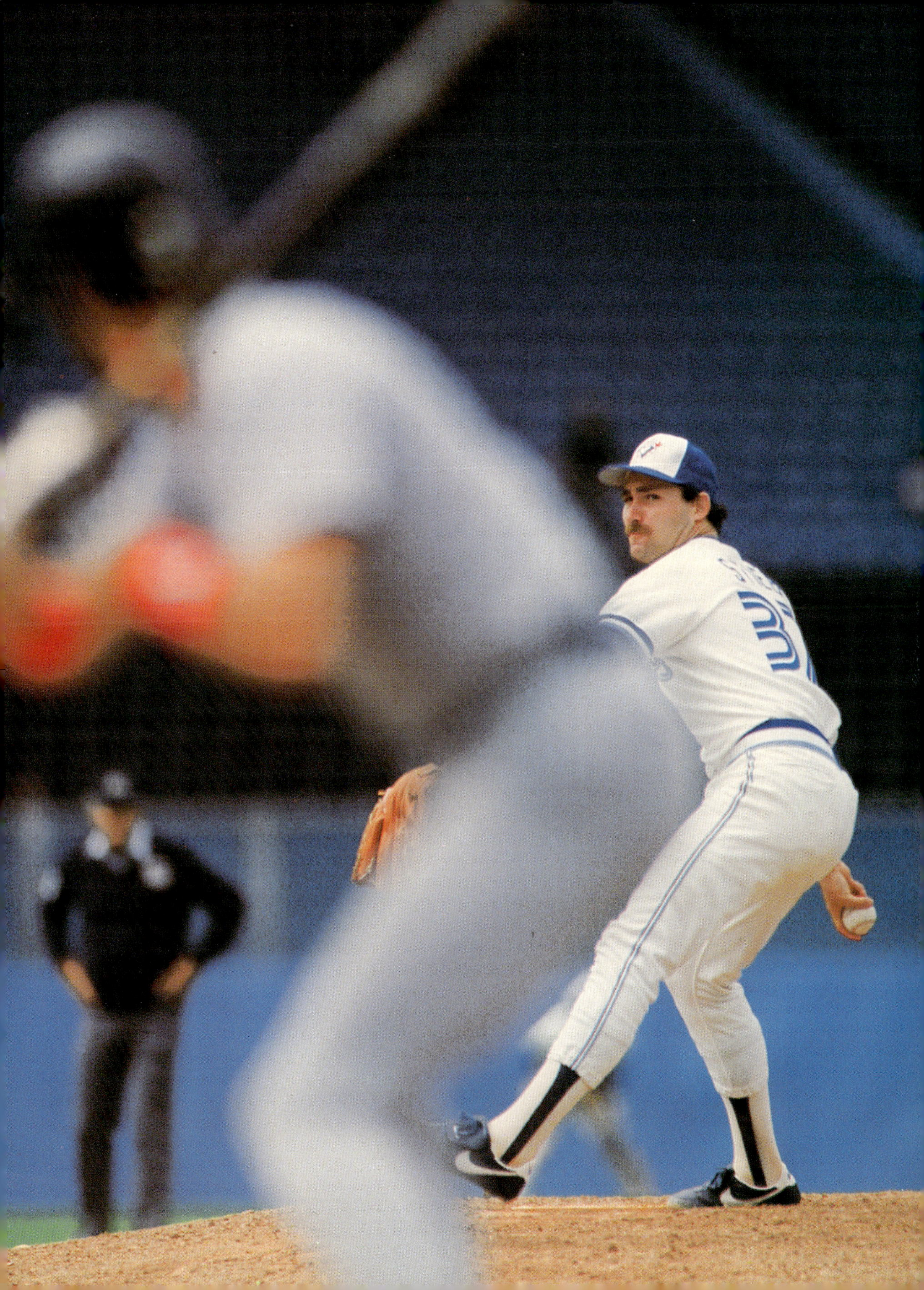

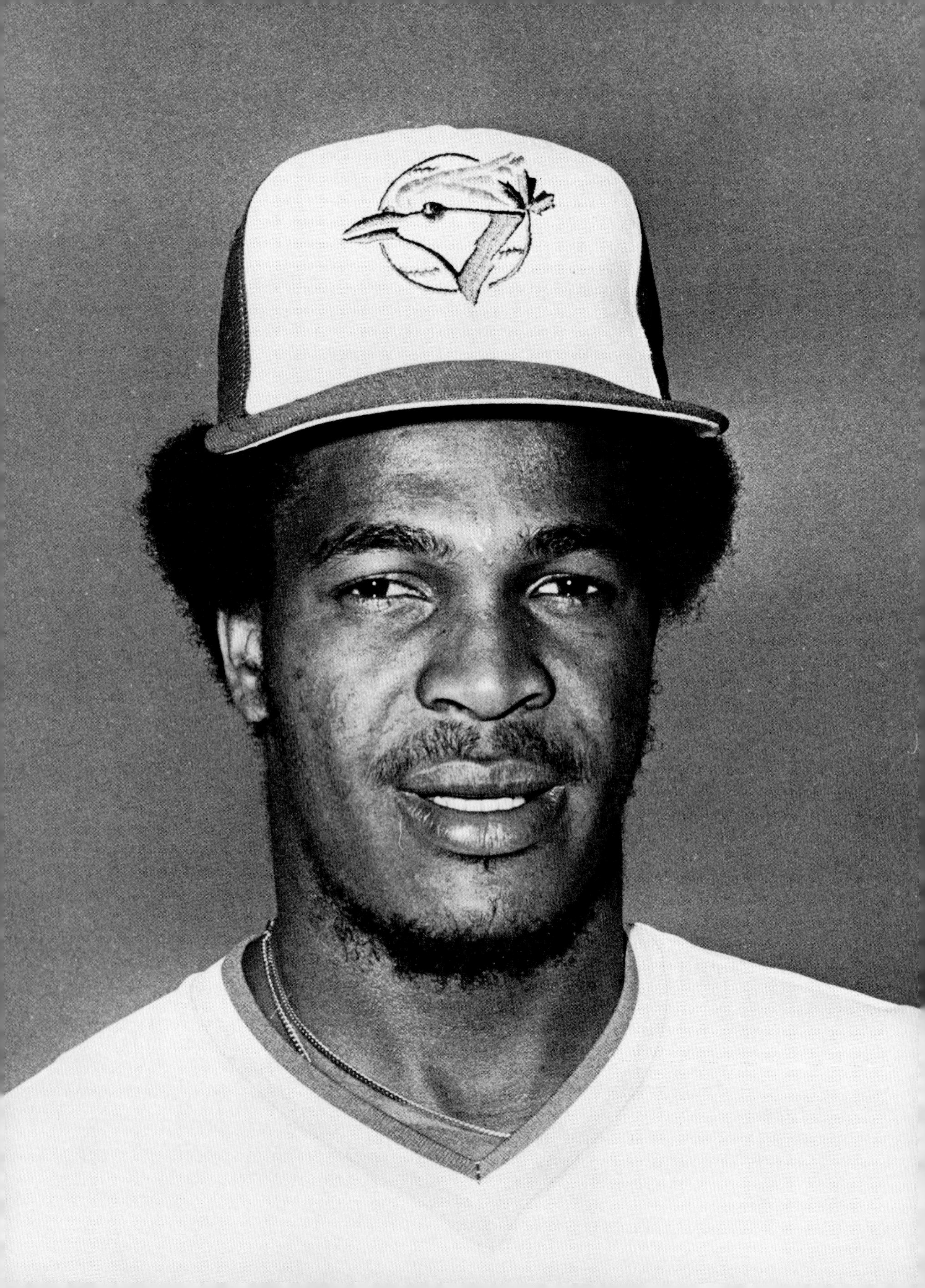

house door and wheels out one nuclear missile after another."

Let's take a look. From the minors have come such potential superstars as Mike Sharperson, Manny Lee, Nelson Liriano, Santiago Garcia, Fred McGriff, Glenallen Hill, Sil Campusano, Rob Ducey, and others.

Now the veterans. Heading into the '87 season, the Toronto outfield featured three of the greatest all-around athletes in the majors.

There was Jesse Barfield who had led the big leagues in 1986 with 40 home runs.

There was leftfielder George Bell, who had launched 31 homers and 15 game-winners in '86. (Together, Barfield and Bell had hit 13 more homers that year than the entire St. Louis Cardinals team!)

And, of course, there was Lloyd Moseby, who was always counted on for 20 homers and 30 stolen bases.

At shortstop stood the indestructible Tony Fernandez — a shoo-in future Hall-of-Famer. In 1986, Fernandez had slashed 213 hits, the most by a shortstop in baseball history, while completing his 327th consecutive game without injury or substitution.

At third stood Kelly Gruber, a 25-year-old banger and base thief who was just coming into his own.

At first stood veteran Willie Upshaw — a fearsome hitter — backed up by young Fred McGriff, a AAA phenom.

"We'll have our starting pitchers back in good shape this year, too," grinned Gillick, referring to Key, Stieb, Clancy and Johnson, backed up by ace relievers Henke and Eichhorn.

1986
Ace reliever Tom Henke sets a new club record with 27 saves.

PHOTO
George Bell roamed the outfield for the Jays during the best days of '82.

**1986
Tony Fernandez
gets 213 hits,
the most by
a shortstop
in baseball
history.**

So much talent. It's bound to happen soon. If an American hockey team can win the Stanley Cup, a Canadian baseball team can win the World Series. What a fine day that will be for the sport we call the "All-American Game!"

**PHOTO
Blue Jay
second baseman
Garth Iorg puts
the glove to
Willie Randolph.
(1986)**